The FREEDOM
of a CHRISTIAN

"*Mark Tranvik has done a favor for all students of the Reformation by providing this eminently readable, fresh translation of Martin Luther's premier Reformation tract, his 1520 'The Freedom of a Christian.' With a marvelous introduction to Luther's thought and helpful notes, this new version of Luther's text will help the present generation of students and teachers, professional and armchair theologians and historians, hear Luther's words from a new perspective.*"

Timothy J. Wengert
Professor of the History of Christianity
Lutheran Theological Seminary at Philadelphia

Lucas Cranach the Elder, *Title border,* woodcut.
Title page of Martin Luther's German version of his
1520 publication, "The Freedom of a Christian."

The FREEDOM *of a* CHRISTIAN

MARTIN LUTHER

Translated and introduced by
Mark D. Tranvik

Fortress Press
Minneapolis

THE FREEDOM OF A CHRISTIAN

Cover design: Nate Salciccioli, The DesignWorks Group
Book design: Jill C. Lafferty
Interior details: Detail on p. 1 of *Wittenberg, 1540*, Holschnitt Meister M.S., woodcut; detail on p. 31 from Matthias Gerung, *Shipwreck of the Catholic Clergy*, 1545, woodcut; detail on p. 47 from Hans Baldung Grier, *Martin Luther with a Nimbus and Dove*, 1521, woodcut.

Library of Congress Cataloging-in-Publication Data
Luther, Martin, 1483-1546.
  [Tractatus de libertate Christiana. English]
  The freedom of a Christian / Martin Luther ; translated and introduced by Mark D. Tranvik.
      p. cm.
  ISBN 978-0-8006-6311-7 (alk. paper)
  1. Liberty—Religious aspects—Christianity. I. Tranvik, Mark D. II. Title.
  BR332.S6L88 2008
  233'.7—dc22
                              2008011150

Manufactured in the U.S.A.

CONTENTS

PREFACE

Martin Luther's work on Christian liberty has long been recognized as one of the classics of the Reformation. His ringing declaration that a Christian is "lord of all, completely free of everything" and a "servant, completely attentive to the needs of all" has echoed through five centuries of history and stimulated numerous discussions on the substance of the faith, what it means to lead a Christian life, and the relationship between the church and the larger society.

There has not been a translation of the longer Latin text (Luther also did a shorter version in German[1]) since Harold Grimm revised the earlier work of H. A. Lambert for the American Edition of *Luther's Works* in 1957. Twenty years of teaching "The Freedom of a Christian" to students and adults convinced me that a new translation was needed. Many of the sentences in Grimm's revision were long and overly complex. Furthermore, the situation of today's reader is different from that of the mid-twentieth century. Few have even a general knowledge of Luther or European history.[2] This has necessitated a basic introduction to Luther's era and the use of many footnotes to explain the historical references and theological concepts in

---

1. Translated by Philip W. Krey in *Luther's Spirituality*, Classics of Western Spirituality, ed. and trans. Philip W. Krey and Peter D. S. Krey (New York: Paulist, 2007), 69–90.

2. Of course, this description does not fit everyone. Those who desire a thorough theological commentary on the text should consult the work of Reinhold Rieger. His *Von der Freiheit eines Christenmenschen. De libertate christiana.* Kommentare zu Schriften Luthers, Band 1 (Tübingen: Mohr Siebeck, 2007) is a model of careful scholarship.

the text. A chronology, map, suggestions for further reading, and a glossary also have been added to aid readers who are entering the world of the sixteenth century for the first time. A list of the abbreviations used in this volume can be found in the back matter. Subject dividers have been used to help the reader follow the flow of Luther's argument. The overall goal is to make one of Luther's most important writings accessible to a new generation of students and readers.

A translation like this is never the work of one individual. A larger community has helped to shape this book, although they are not to be held accountable for any errors it may contain. My deepest gratitude goes out to the following groups and individuals: the Religion Department at Augsburg College, Augsburg College's Lilly Scholars of 2006–2007, and Diane Glorvigen, the program associate for Augsburg's Lilly Endowment grant on vocation. A special thanks to Scott Hendrix, Robert Kolb, and Eugene Skibbe. All three reviewed my translation of "The Freedom of a Christian" and made numerous suggestions that improved the text. Thanks to Marissa Bauck and Michael West, editors at Fortress Press.

CHRONOLOGY OF MARTIN LUTHER'S LIFE

1483 — Born in Eisleben, Germany

1501 — Enters the University of Erfurt

1505 — Earns Master of Arts degree

Thunderstorm and entrance into monastery in Erfurt

1507 — Ordination into priesthood

1512 — Becomes Doctor of Theology

Begins teaching at University of Wittenberg

OCT. 31

1517 — Posts "The Ninety-five Theses"

1518 — Sylvester Prierias writes against "The Ninety-five Theses"

Heidelberg Disputation

Meets with Cardinal Cajetan in Augsburg

1519 — Debates with John Eck in Leipzig

1520 — Papal bull threatening excommunication

The Five Treatises of 1520:
"Treatise on Good Works"
"The Papacy in Rome, An Answer to the Celebrated Romanist in Leipzig"
"To the Christian Nobility of the German Nation"
"The Babylonian Captivity of the Church"
"The Freedom of a Christian"

1521 — Diet of Worms: Luther's Expulsion from the Roman Catholic Church

1521–22 — Luther in the Wartburg Castle

1525 — Peasants' Rebellion

Luther is married to Katherine von Bora

1530 — The Augsburg Confession

1546 — Luther dies in Eisleben, Germany

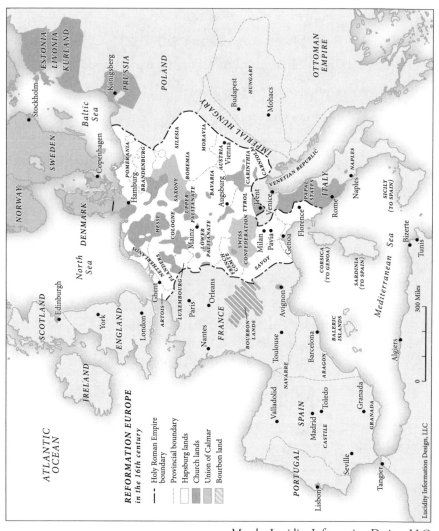

REFORMATION EUROPE
in the 16th century

Holy Roman Empire boundary
Provincial boundary
Hapsburg lands
Church lands
Union of Calmar
Bourbon land

Map by Lucidity Information Design, LLC

ATLANTIC OCEAN

IRELAND

SCOTLAND
Edinburgh

ENGLAND
York
London

NORWAY

SWEDEN
Stockholm

North Sea

Baltic Sea

DENMARK
Copenhagen

ESTONIA
LIVONIA
KURLAND

Königsberg
PRUSSIA

POLAND

NETHERLANDS
Ghent
FLANDERS
ARTOIS
LUXEMBOURG
Paris
Orleans
Nantes

FRANCE

BOURBON LANDS

POMERANIA
Hamburg
BRANDENBURG
HESSE
COLOGNE
Mainz
SAXONY
UPPER PALATINATE
LOWER PALATINATE
SILESIA
BOHEMIA
MORAVIA
AUSTRIA
Vienna
BAVARIA
Augsburg
SWISS CONFEDERATION
FRANCHE COMTÉ
SAVOY
Milan
Pavia
Genoa
Trent
CARINTHIA
CARNIOLA
IMPERIAL HUNGARY
Budapest
HUNGARY
Mohacs

VENETIAN REPUBLIC
Venice
Florence
PAPAL STATES
Rome
ITALY
NAPLES
Naples
SICILY (TO SPAIN)

CORSICA (TO GENOA)
SARDINIA (TO SPAIN)

Avignon
Toulouse
NAVARRE
Barcelona
ARAGON
BALERIC ISLANDS

Mediterranean Sea

Bizerte
Tunis
Algiers

SPAIN
Valladolid
Madrid
CASTILE
Toledo
Granada
GRANADA
Seville

PORTUGAL
Lisbon

Tangier

OTTOMAN EMPIRE

0   300 Miles

Lucidity Information Design, LLC

MARTIN LUTHER'S ROAD TO FREEDOM

A Survey of His Early Life and Teaching

He has redeemed me, a lost and condemned human being.
He has purchased and freed me from all sins, from death,
and from the power of the devil, not with gold or silver but
with his holy, precious blood and with his innocent suffer-
ing and death.[1]

Martin Luther wrote these words for his Small Catechism in 1528. He was explaining to his readers the liberating power of Jesus Christ's death on the cross. It is the pivotal sentence in the most influential book that Luther ever wrote.[2] These words serve as a useful starting point for those wishing to understand the man who shaped and directed the first wave of the Protestant Reformation. If we can obtain insight on what Luther meant by being freed "from all sins, from death, and from the power of the devil," then we also shall have gained a perspective that will bring his treatise "The Freedom of a Christian" into clearer focus.

A World of Sin, Death, and the Devil

The sixteenth-century world of Martin Luther was dominated by a fear of death that we scarcely can appreciate today. A person had to be prepared for death, for it could strike with very little warning. In the middle of the 1300s, Europe suffered from a cruel and brutal attack of the bubonic plague. According to some estimates, over a third of Europe's population died from this highly contagious disease. The plague did not distinguish between its victims, striking both rich and poor, noble and peasant,

---

1. Martin Luther, The Small Catechism, in *BC* 355.

2. Charles P. Arand, *That I May Be His Own: An Overview of Luther's Catechisms* (St. Louis: Concordia, 2000), 15.

city-dweller and rural villager. It would visit the continent repeatedly over the next four hundred years, including an outbreak in Luther's own German town of Wittenberg in 1527.[3]

Even in areas free of the plague, death was hardly a stranger. Infant mortality rates were exceptionally high, to say nothing of the many dangers accompanying women in childbirth. Famine, disease, war, and a poor diet combined to ensure that most people living in Luther's day would not see many years beyond their fortieth birthday.

There is also substantial evidence that the popular piety and official teaching of the church in this time tended to increase the fear of death with an extremely vengeful and judgmental understanding of God. Christ often was pictured in sermons and pamphlets as the judge coming on the rainbow at the end of time (see Matt. 25:31-46).[4] In this great day of reckoning, he would separate the sheep from the goats according to the good deeds done in earthly life. The message for the average person was clear: Be ready to die—it could happen at any moment!—and give an account of your life to this supreme and severe judge.

Of course, we should be careful to balance this view of a harsh and demanding God with the church's understanding of grace. People were not left helpless and alone in the face of death and the demands of Christ. God's grace was made available to Christians through the sacrament of penance. Basically, going to confession (which was required annually and encouraged frequently) involved three steps. First, a person was required to confess all of his or her known sins. A priest, often with the aid of a confessional manual, attempted to scrutinize the penitent's conscience in order to reveal the depth of sin. This process could

---

3. Carter Lindberg, *The European Reformations* (Oxford: Blackwell, 1996), 27–30.

4. Roland Bainton, *Here I Stand: A Life of Martin Luther* (Nashville: Abingdon, 1950), 22.

be burdensome and even perverse. Second, following the confession of sins, the priest would pronounce absolution. Third, the penitent would be asked to do a work of satisfaction that was roughly equivalent to the sins he or she had committed. Having completed penance, a Christian then could go to the Eucharist (or worship service where Holy Communion was served) and receive the body and blood of Christ with a good conscience.

The sacrament of penance was where the church intersected with the daily lives of people in a highly significant way. In theory, it should have been the place where God's grace was made available to people burdened by sin and frightened of death. But there is a lot of evidence to suggest that it did not work that way.[5] Sometimes the act of confession required such a lengthy and detailed recounting of sins that it virtually drowned out the voice of the priest pronouncing absolution. In other words, some found it difficult to hear the church's word of forgiveness after an exhausting investigation of their own unworthiness.

Also in connection with penance, there arose the practice of selling indulgences. These documents were authorized by the church and could be substituted for the third part of penance, the work of satisfaction. Instead of doing the prescribed acts of penance (prayers or a visit to a shrine, for example), it was possible to buy an indulgence that would satisfy the final part of the sacrament of penance. Originally, this was meant to cover the temporal punishment of sins that were already forgiven. But in Luther's day many were led by the church to believe they were purchasing forgiveness itself.[6] Indulgences could be expensive, especially when they contained extravagant claims like promising to return the purchaser to the state of spiritual innocence that she enjoyed in baptism. We will visit the issue of indulgences

---

5. Steven Ozment, *The Age of Reform, 1250–1550* (New Haven: Yale University Press, 1980), 219–22.

6. *ER* II:314–15.

Matthias Gerung, *Sale of Indulgences,* 1546, woodcut.

again when we talk about the first stages of Luther's public rebellion against the church.

The fear of death and the dread of sin were but manifestations of a larger and darker power that haunted all of medieval life: the devil. It is tempting for modern people to dismiss the devil as a cartoon character or as a sinister but fictional force in horror films and novels. But Luther lived in a time that believed intensely in the reality of the devil. Indeed, Luther considered

him as the chief adversary of Christ and faith.[7] Sin and death
had the power to terrify, but they were mere manifestations of
Satan, the dark, shrewd, and insidious power that attempted to
wrest fragile souls away from God's embrace. Luther's battles
with the devil were real and personal and, as the following passages show, often involved Satan's attempt to snare the Reformer's
conscience:

> When I awoke last night, the Devil came and wanted to debate
> with me; he rebuked and reproached me, arguing that I was a
> sinner. To this I replied: Tell me something new, Devil! I already
> know that perfectly well; I have committed many a solid and
> real sin. Indeed there must be good honest sins—not fabricated
> and invented ones—for God to forgive for his beloved Son's
> sake, who took all my sins upon Him so that now the sins I have
> committed are no longer mine but belong to Christ. This won-
> derful gift of God I am not prepared to deny (in my response to
> the Devil), but want to acknowledge and confess.[8]

In summary, when Luther speaks in his Small Catechism
of being "freed from all sins, from death, and from the power
of the devil," he is not simply reciting theological abstractions
culled from dusty textbooks. Sin, death, and the devil repre-
sented for him a diabolical trinity that haunted every corner
of late medieval life. To a degree unimaginable to the modern
Western mind, death was a regular and frequent feature of daily

---

7. Heiko Oberman makes this observation about Luther and the devil: "Luther's
world of thought is wholly distorted and apologetically misconstrued if his con-
ception of the Devil is dismissed as a medieval phenomenon and only his faith
in Christ retained as relevant or as the only decisive factor. Christ and the Devil
were equally real to him: one was the perpetual intercessor for Christianity, the
other a menace to mankind till the end. To argue that Luther never overcame the
medieval belief in the Devil says far too little; he even intensified it and lent to it
additional urgency: Christ and Satan wage a cosmic war for mastery over Church
and world." Heiko Oberman, *Luther: Man between God and the Devil*, trans.
Eileen Walliser-Schwarzbart (New Haven: Yale University Press, 1989), 104.

8. *WATr* 6:215–16 as translated in Oberman, *Luther*, 105–106.

existence. Furthermore, death was not seen as happenstance or accidental; as the Christian Bible instructed, it was the fruit of sin. And finally, the force responsible for all this physical and spiritual havoc was none other than the devil himself.

Luther's Early Years

Martin Luther was born in a region of present-day northern Germany that was known in the sixteenth century as Saxony. The German national boundaries that are familiar to us did not come into existence until the latter part of the nineteenth century. In Luther's day "Germany" was actually a patchwork of semi-autonomous cities, states, and principalities that made up a region called the Holy Roman Empire. Saxony was a relatively powerful and influential part of the Empire. Its ruler would later play an important role in Luther's life and in the course of the Reformation.

Luther's birthplace was Eisleben, a small village near an area of copper mines. Luther's father, Hans, was a miner, and throughout his life Luther would make references to his humble beginnings. His parents were strict, but the discipline administered at home was generally well within the bounds of sixteenth-century standards. There was sufficient prosperity to allow Luther to attend school, and he seems to have thrived at each stage of his education. His instruction began in Mansfeld and continued in Magdeburg and Eisenach. In 1501, at the age of seventeen, he entered the University of Erfurt. At this point he seems eager to follow the wishes of his father that he become a lawyer.

It is not hard to speculate why Hans Luther would desire such a future for his son. A career in law undoubtedly seemed more attractive than the hard life of a miner. Furthermore, if Luther was eventually hired by the Saxon court or by some other branch of the nobility, it would bring renown to the family

Albrecht Dürer, Title woodcut to *Wie der Würfell auf ist kumen,* 1489, woodcut. Above: the devil tempts a knight to gamble, and a fight at the gaming table results in the punishment of death on the wheel. Below: executions resulting from gambling.

name. Finally, the financial rewards from being a lawyer might mean an easier life for the parents in their old age.

Luther received his master's degree from the University of Erfurt in 1505. He immediately began to study law but then abruptly entered an austere Augustinian monastery in Erfurt. Later on in life he would describe this drastic change of direction as the result of a near-death experience in a thunderstorm just outside Erfurt. Fearing for his life as the lightning flashed nearby, he appealed to St. Ann, patron saint of miners, and vowed to enter the cloister if he survived the storm. The storm passed and Luther, determined to make good on his pledge, left his law studies behind and entered the monastery to become a friar.

Luther's daily routine in the monastery was carefully prescribed.[9] A schedule was followed for when to eat, pray, worship, study, and sleep. As Luther progressed through the first year (the novitiate), he was recognized by his superiors as a good student and was eventually put on a track to be a teacher. But the main purpose of the monastery was the formation of Luther's soul. The disciplines he followed were designed to mold him to the image of Christ. Monks took seriously the command of Christ to take up their crosses and follow him. Accordingly, they committed themselves to lives of poverty, chastity, and obedience. This included regular worship (seven times per day following the canonical hours), fasting, prayers, and the frequent examination of their consciences.

Luther's monastery was especially strict. The monks strove for an astonishingly high ideal: to love God absolutely and to practice perfect humility.[10] Note what is being required in these commands. God is not to be loved for any self-serving reasons. For example, a love of God that sought to avoid punishment would be an inferior devotion, because it was done for selfish

---

9. For more information on Luther's experience in the monastery, see James Kittelson, *Luther the Reformer: The Story of the Man and His Career* (Minneapolis: Fortress Press, 1986), 51–63.

10. Walther von Loewenich, *Martin Luther: The Man and His Work*, trans. Lawrence W. Denef (Minneapolis: Augsburg, 1986), 73.

reasons. Rather, God was to be loved absolutely (no other motives allowed!) because that is what should be rendered to the almighty Lord of the universe. This is fine in theory but could lead to troubling spiritual conclusions when put into practice. In Luther's case it led to a level of uncertainty that caused him to believe he was worthy of eternal damnation.

For Luther the crisis came to a head in his relationship with his beloved confessor, Johannes von Staupitz. Concerned to confess all his known sins, Luther wearied Staupitz with the revelations of his scrupulous conscience. Despite his confessor's attempt to console him, Luther found himself in the midst of a frightening downward spiral in his relationship to God. No matter how hard he tried, he could not seem to do enough to please God. A large issue here was the theology that Luther had been taught. He believed it was necessary that he take the first step in his relationship with God; once this initial act was done, God would reward the effort with grace. But Luther was never satisfied that he had done enough. When it came to confessing his sins, Luther's experience was one of bondage, not liberation:

> When I was a monk, I made a great effort to live according to the requirements of the monastic rule. I made a practice of confessing and reciting all my sins, but always with prior contrition; I went to confession frequently, and I performed the assigned penances faithfully. Nevertheless, my conscience could never achieve certainty but was always in doubt and said, "You have not done this correctly. You were not contrite enough. You omitted this in your confession."[11]

The longer Luther lived as a monk, the more he was haunted by his doubts and failings. His inability to achieve salvation resulted in an intense trial known by the German word *Anfechtung*.

---

11. "Lectures on Galatians, 1535," *WA* 40(2):15; *LW* 27:15.

There is no precise English equivalent, but *Anfechtung* can be described as an experience of doubt and despair that pierces the very soul—far more than a case of "the blues." *Anfechtung* points to a profound sense of being lost, alienated, and out of control. It is tempting by today's standards to "psychologize" Luther and suggest he suffered from depression. This may be true, but for Luther it was not something happening only within his psyche. The battle was with an external foe: the almighty God himself. Luther was convinced that God had turned against him and was even actively assaulting him with his judgment and wrath. This struggle was not continuous, as that would have been unbearable. But Luther was also not able to shake *Anfechtung*. As yet another manifestation of the devil, it lurked nearby, seeking to rob him of faith and peace. The net result was a great irony. Luther entered the monastery seeking salvation but ended up convinced that he was condemned.

Luther's Radical God

At this point, it is important to introduce a conversation partner that accompanied Luther during his years in the monastery: the Bible. As mentioned earlier, Luther was encouraged by his superiors to become a teacher. This sense of calling led him to become a student of the Scriptures, and he eventually earned his doctorate in 1512 and became a theology professor at the University of Wittenberg. At first the Bible only aggravated his bouts with *Anfechtung*. Many biblical passages simply reminded him of God's role as judge and of his own unworthiness. Even Christ was more likely to be seen as the fearful final arbiter in the last judgment rather than the merciful savior of sinners: "I was often terrified before the name of Jesus . . . When his name was spoken I would rather have heard the devil mentioned, for

I thought I would have to do good works until by them Christ had been made my gracious friend."[12]

But eventually, he came to read the Bible in a different way. Scholars long have debated the precise date on which Luther experienced his so-called breakthrough. It is probably more accurate to say that over a period of years he began to see God in a new light. From the perspective of a timeline, we know that Luther lacked the new insight in 1513 but had obtained it by 1518. Just what happened during those years?

For one thing, Luther began to read the Apostle Paul's writings in a new way, particularly his letter to the Romans and his teaching that a "person is justified by faith apart from works prescribed by the law" (Rom. 3:28). Previously, Luther believed that God's righteousness was something he had to attain (always aided by grace, of course); however, his experience in the monastery demonstrated the limitations of that view. Now he comes to see Paul as saying that God actually *gives* his righteousness to those who do not deserve it: "For there is no distinction, since all have sinned and fall short of the glory of God; they are now justified by his grace as a gift" (Rom. 3:22-24). Late in his life, Luther provided his own account of this period. It is worth quoting at some length as long as we keep in mind that he was looking back some thirty years to a tumultuous time:

> Though I lived as a monk without reproach, I felt that I was a sinner before God with an extremely disturbed conscience. I could not believe that he was placated by my satisfaction. I did not love, yes, I hated the righteous God who punishes sinners, and secretly, if not blasphemously, certainly murmuring greatly, I was angry with God. . . . At last, by the mercy of God, meditating day and night, I gave heed to the context of the words,

12. *WA* 47:590 as quoted in von Loewenich, 77.

namely, "In it the righteousness of God is revealed, as it is written, 'He who through faith is righteous shall live.'" There I began to understand that the righteousness of God is that by which the righteous lives by a gift of God, namely by faith. And this is the meaning: the righteousness of God is revealed by the gospel, namely, the passive righteousness with which merciful God justifies us by faith. . . . Here I felt that I was altogether born again and had entered paradise itself through open gates.[13]

Further light can be shed on Luther's new understanding of God by following his interpretation of the Psalms. We know that Luther regularly meditated on the Psalms, and we have many commentaries on them from this crucial span of years. Luther prized the Psalms especially for the way they expressed the highs and lows of the life of faith. They also helped him to clarify the meaning of Jesus' death on the cross. For example, while reflecting on Psalm 22, Luther was struck by the first verse: "My God, my God, why have you forsaken me?"[14] These were the very words used by Christ during his crucifixion. Luther began to ponder: Why would Christ utter this cry of dereliction? He recognized it was not only a cry of pain but the shriek of someone who had been abandoned and deserted. Luther puzzled over why Christ would feel the very *Anfechtungen* that had plagued him in the monastery. It just did not seem to make sense. After all, Christ had loved God absolutely. His devotion to God had been pure. It was not diluted with self-interest and mixed motives, like Luther's imperfect love.

Luther's view of the cross began to change when he realized that Christ's cry or scream was the result of bearing human sin. Christ himself had not committed sin; he voluntarily took upon himself the entire sin of the world. This was not done only in a

---

13. "Preface to Latin Writings, 1535," *WA* 54:185–86; *LW* 34:336–37.

14. See Bainton, *Here I Stand*, 47.

Albrecht Dürer, *Christ on the Cross,* 1516, woodcut.

conceptual or theoretical way. Christ really and truly took sin upon himself, as if he had committed them in the first place.[15] We might ask ourselves: What would it feel like to be responsible for the world's sin? Of course, it is far beyond the power of our imaginations to conceive of such a thing. After all, who

15. An excellent introduction to this idea can be found in Robert W. Bertram, "Luther on the Unique Mediatorship of Christ," in *The One Mediator, the Saints, and Mary: Lutherans and Catholics in Dialogue VIII*, ed. H. George Anderson, J. Francis Stafford, and Joseph Burgess, 249–62 (Minneapolis: Augsburg Fortress, 1992).

would want to have the conscience of a concentration camp guard or a child abuser? We struggle enough with our own guilt and shortcomings and certainly would not want the "baggage" of someone else's life. But in Luther's view this is precisely what happened on the cross, and it led directly to his new understanding of Christian freedom.

Luther's next step was to take the "logic" of the cross and apply it to his own situation. If Christ has the world's sin on himself, then Luther's own sin is on Christ as well. If Luther's sin is borne by Christ, then he (Luther) is free of sin. If he is free of sin, then he is righteous. The very thing that Luther tried to obtain by all his labors in the monastery was given to him freely in Christ. Luther termed this the "happy exchange," whereby Christ, out of love, traded his righteousness and purity to sinners and received from them their guilt and shame. It is a terribly "unjust" exchange, since our sin kills Christ while his righteousness yields life and freedom for undeserving sinners. But it is all accomplished by God in Christ by a remarkable and radical act of love.

It is tempting in an introduction like this to telescope and flatten what is undoubtedly a complicated and uneven period in Luther's life. What has been said above about Luther's rediscovery of the gospel should be supplemented by the understanding that Luther's insights were the result of years of struggle, argument, discussion, and anguish. However, for our purposes we do know that something dramatic had changed by 1517 or 1518: an intense engagement with the Bible resulted in a fresh and bracing interpretation of the Christian faith. It might be useful to follow the Lutheran tradition at this point and summarize Luther's new theology under the following phrases: *grace alone, faith alone,* and *Christ alone.*

First, Luther's theology put an emphasis on grace alone. He came to understand grace as an active power from God that communicates God's love to us. The "alone" is important because it stresses that God's grace does not need any works to complete it. Luther was surrounded by traditions and practices in the late medieval church that suggested we had to do certain things to qualify for grace, or we at least had to cooperate with grace. Luther became convinced that any attempt to combine works with grace ends up undermining grace and glorifying human effort.

Second, God's grace has the power to change human beings or to transform them into people who trust God. Thus there is an emphasis in Luther's theology on faith alone. Again, note the "alone." Faith is sufficient—it does not need to be completed by any human works. Furthermore, Luther was careful not to limit faith to mere "belief." Faith is more than intellectual assent to certain ideas or propositions. For example, simply to mouth the words of the Apostles' Creed is not the same thing as faith. Luther understood faith as "trust," something that embraced the whole self—the heart and the body as well as the mind. The difference between belief and trust might be likened to the difference between knowing the definition of a mother and having a mom. The former is purely intellectual and is knowledge anyone could have. The latter involves a relationship and presumably implies years of love, nurture, and care. The ability to trust is supplied by God, who works in us through the power of his Holy Spirit. In 1528 Luther's explanation to the third article of the Apostle's Creed in his Small Catechism underlines this teaching: "I believe that by my own understanding or strength I cannot believe in Jesus Christ my Lord or come to him, but instead the Holy Spirit has called me through the gospel, enlightened me with his gifts, made me holy, and kept me in the true faith. . . ."[16]

Finally, grace alone and faith alone are possible because of what Christ alone did on the cross. The "happy exchange"

---

16. Small Catechism, in *BC* 355.

discussed above means that the righteousness necessary before God has been given to us by Christ. This is wholly God's act on our behalf, and we can add nothing to it. When talking about Christ, Luther often uses the image of a marriage, as he does in "The Freedom of a Christian." When two people get married they end up sharing each other's property. In financial terms, the debts and assets of the groom become those of the bride and vice versa. Luther suggests that a similar thing happens when the sinner is joined to Christ by the "wedding ring" of faith. All of Christ's righteousness and innocence are transferred to his bride while he receives shame and guilt from her. The result of this union is a Christ laden with sin and a Christian made pure and righteous.

The triad of grace, faith, and Christ alone rest on Scripture. But care needs to be taken when talking about Luther's views on the Bible. From the time he began lecturing in 1513 as a newly minted doctor of theology until his death in 1546, many of his waking hours were spent poring over the meaning of biblical texts; however, strange as it may seem, the Bible for him was never an end in itself. The center or heart of Scripture is the proclamation of Christ, crucified and risen, all for the sake of human sinners. Luther knew very well that his opponents also took the Bible very seriously. It was not the authority of the Bible as such that drove him to challenge the teachings of his day. Rather, it was the Christ revealed in Scripture that fueled his new way of thinking. This was not an attempt to degrade the Bible's authority. Indeed, for Luther this way of thinking enhanced the Scriptures because it is only through them that one encounters this God who through Christ justifies the ungodly (Rom. 5:5).

Luther Goes Public

We need to return to Luther's life story. We have traced the development of his theological revolution while he was in the monastery. His first seven years (1505–1512) as a friar also witnessed his ordination to the priesthood (1507) and his reception of a doctorate degree (1512) that qualified him to be a professor of the Bible. The latter is particularly important because to the end of his life Luther understood his vocation as one called to interpret the Scriptures for the church. In the same year that he received his degree, he was sent to the German city that would be intertwined with his name for the rest of his days: Wittenberg.

As a professor at the University of Wittenberg, Luther expounded for his students the meaning of the various books of the Bible. From 1513 to 1518 we have his lectures on the Psalms, Romans, Galatians, and Hebrews. As noted above, these years were decisive in the formation of his new theological sensibilities. Luther was also more than an academic. He was a preacher in Wittenberg's church. But Luther was not content to remain in the classroom or the pulpit. As he cast his eye on the practices of his church, he became convinced that he needed to call attention to a community that had strayed from the core teachings of the Scriptures.

The immediate object of his wrath was the sale of indulgences. In order to understand what happened, it is necessary to take a brief excursion into the complicated world of sixteenth-century ecclesiastical politics. Pope Leo X authorized a sale of indulgences in northern Germany for the purposes of raising money to build St. Peter's basilica in Rome. Actually, the indulgences were not sold in Wittenberg itself because they would have competed with the money attracted by the elaborate relic collection of Frederick the Wise, the prince of electoral Saxony. But they were available in villages and towns close to Wittenberg, and some of Luther's parishioners purchased them. This incensed Luther because the underlying theological rationale of indulgences suggested that God's grace could be purchased.

He responded with a protest document known as "The Ninety-five Theses," which he posted on the door of the Castle

Hans Brosamer, *Martin Luther in the Pulpit,* woodcut.

Church in Wittenberg in 1517. They were written in Latin, the
academic language of the day, and were intended to provoke a
debate within the university. They did much more than that.
Within months, remarkably fast by sixteenth-century standards,
they were translated into German and distributed throughout
the cities and universities of northern Europe.[17] Suddenly, Luther
no longer was an obscure monk teaching in a backwater Saxon
university. His name was now on the minds and lips of the day's
leading theologians, scholars, and church people.

"The Ninety-five Theses" sparked debate because they
attacked the church's understanding of penance. The first two
theses make Luther's argument clear: (1) "When our Lord and
Master Jesus Christ said, 'Repent' (Matt. 4:17), he willed the

---

17. For the importance of printing, see Mark U. Edwards, *Printing, Propaganda,
and Martin Luther* (Minneapolis: Fortress Press, 2006 [1994]).

entire life of believers to be one of repentance." (2) "This word cannot be understood as referring to the sacrament of penance, that is, confession and satisfaction, as administered by the clergy."[18] As explained earlier, the late medieval church had much invested in the sacrament of penance. It was a key intersection between the institution and the life of a late-medieval Christian—a place where he or she sought refuge from the tyranny of "sin, death, and the devil." Laypeople assumed that in order to be in a right relationship with God it was necessary to partake in the church's ritual of confession; however, in the "The Ninety-five Theses," Luther called this entire worldview into question. He claimed that confession should not be understood within the narrow confines of the sacrament of penance. Rather, repentance is a continual and repeated part of the Christian life and should not be relegated to a formal relationship with a church and a priest. From Luther's perspective, the life of faith involves a constant battle with the devil. Repentance needs to take place daily, even hourly, in this new understanding. Relegating it to a sacramental practice simply does not do justice to Satan's tenacity and the fragility of faith.

Not only did Luther attack the understanding of penance in "The Ninety-five Theses," but he also criticized the practice of selling indulgences that had come to be associated with this sacrament. He made clear that people cannot be reconciled to God through the purchase of indulgences (Thesis 33). Moreover, he suggested that love of neighbor and giving money to the poor are better uses of a Christian's time and resources than the purchase of indulgences (Thesis 43).[19]

The indulgence controversy opened a gap between Luther and Rome. A series of representatives from the pope would now

---

18. Luther, "Ninety-five Theses, 1517," *WA* 1:233; *LW* 31:25

19. Ibid., *WA* 1:235; *LW* 31:28–29.

attempt to mediate the dispute; however, all efforts to bring the two sides closer together failed. In fact, the opposite occurred. Each time Luther was challenged, he tended to become more radical in his assessment of the church's teachings. By 1520, some three years after his critique of indulgences, Luther would challenge the fundamental assumptions of papal authority.

The first figure to respond to "The Ninety-five Theses" was an Italian named Sylvester Mazzolini, known better as Prierias. He wrote a "Dialogue against the Arrogant Theses of Martin Luther concerning the Power of the Pope." As the title of the work suggests, it was basically a reassertion of papal power. In other words, Luther's position was wrong because the pope said so. Prierias's writing also became the basis for the pope's demand that Luther appear in Rome and defend himself against the charge of heresy.

At this point, Luther appealed to his prince, Frederick the Wise. We have neither time nor space to provide a detailed explanation of the complex political context; however, Frederick the Wise proved to be a dependable patron and protector of Luther. Some of his support can be attributed to the pride that he took in his University of Wittenberg and thus his reluctance to expose his now-famous professor to a tribunal hundreds of miles from Saxony. Frederick arranged for Luther to be examined in Germany instead. In October of 1518 Luther met with Cardinal Cajetan in Augsburg. Expecting a dialogue, Luther was shocked to discover that Cajetan was not interested in conversation, only in a recantation of his teaching. The meeting ended abruptly with Luther escaping from Augsburg under the cover of darkness.

Another event occurred in 1518 that was crucial in Luther's theological development: the Heidelberg Disputation. At a meeting for Augustinian monks, Luther offered a series of theses for debate that contained his radical ideas about law, good works, and the freedom of the will. He made clear his rejection of scholastic theology which is now termed a "theology of glory" in contrast to a biblical "theology of the cross."[20] Several future reformers were present at the disputation and highly impressed by Luther's proposals. These included Martin Bucer, who would later lead the reform in Strassbourg, and Johannes Brenz, who would be an influential Lutheran in southern Germany.

Returning to our overview of the political drama between Luther and Rome, the next person to enter the fray was John Eck, professor of theology at Ingolstadt. Eck challenged Luther's colleague at Wittenberg, Andreas Karlstadt, to a debate in Leipzig. The disputation finally took place in July of 1519. After Eck and Karlstadt disputed for a week, Luther entered the ring. Eck, a learned and clever debater, was able to get Luther to admit that the real subject was not the question of indulgences but rather the issue of ultimate authority in the church. Luther had now moved to the position of challenging the primacy of Rome. An intensive study of early Christianity convinced him that the pope's claim to have the last word was fairly recent and not rooted in the ancient tradition of the church. Moreover, in the course of his arguments with Eck, he also admitted that popes and councils of the church were capable of error. The Leipzig Debate was a public demonstration of how far Luther had strayed from Roman understandings of authority. It also set up an inevitable collision between the Wittenberg reformer and the ecclesiastical establishment.

Following Leipzig, Eck went to Rome and helped compose the case against this German monk who soon would be declared a heretic. Meanwhile, the monk himself entered

---

20. See Martin Luther, "The Heidelberg Disputation, 1518" *WA* 1:353–74; *LW* 31:35–70. An excellent commentary on the disputation is found in Gerhard Forde, *On Being a Theologian of the Cross: Reflections on Luther's Heidelberg Disputation, 1518* (Grand Rapids: Eerdmans, 1997).

into a remarkably fruitful period of writing. During the year 1520, Luther penned three[21] of his most famous treatises: "To the Christian Nobility of the German Nation concerning the Reform of the Christian Estate,"[22] "The Babylonian Captivity of the Church,"[23] and "The Freedom of a Christian." All three writings reflect the confidence of a soul freed by the belief that we are justified by grace through faith alone and not by our works, efforts, or human achievements. In particular, the first two pieces are also strong criticisms of a church and culture that have strayed far from this anchor.

"The Freedom of a Christian" differs in that it is less polemical. It did not attempt to reform an institution or practice but rather sought to establish a framework for the Christian faith. As the reader will see (pp. 31–45), the treatise is actually appended to a letter that Luther sent to Pope Leo X. This epistle deserves careful consideration. It is at once arresting and moving. Luther addresses Pope Leo almost casually at times, as if he were speaking to an equal who has been unwittingly duped by his close associates. But Luther also evidences a deep concern for the state of the church and the pope as a person. Toward the end of the letter, Luther announces his intention to provide Leo with a "summary of the Christian life." What follows is "The Freedom of a Christian" and Luther's conviction that we have been liberated by God for attentive service in the world.

Luther's writings in 1520 only inflamed his terribly strained relationship with Rome. "To the Christian Nobility" questioned

---

21. A strong argument can be made that there were actually five writings in 1520 that were crucial in the development of Luther's theology. In addition to the three named above, *The Papacy in Rome: An Answer to the Celebrated Romanist in Leipzig* (WA 6:285–325; LW 39:55–104) and the *Treatise on Good Works* (WA 6:202–296; LW 44:17–114) are important texts on the church and ethics, respectively.

22. WA 6:404–69; LW 44:123–217.

23. WA 6:497–573; LW 36:11–126.

the church-state nexus that had dominated Europe for almost a millennium. "The Babylonian Captivity of the Church" undercut the sacramental structure that was fundamental to Rome's self-understanding. The momentum generated by these texts coupled with Rome's earlier opposition to Luther meant that he would be excommunicated from the church. Luther defended his teaching before the political and ecclesiastical elite in Worms in 1521. His dramatic testimony concluded with the defiant words: "Unless I am convinced by the testimony of the Scriptures or by clear reason (for I do not trust either in the pope or in councils alone, since it is well known that they have often erred and contradicted themselves), I am bound by the Scriptures I have quoted and my conscience is captive to the Word of God. I cannot and I will not retract anything, since it is neither safe nor right to go against conscience . . . may God help me. Amen."[24]

Sometimes these defiant words have been misinterpreted as a trumpet call for individual autonomy and the right of human beings to be governed by conscience rather than an oppressive structure like the medieval church. Luther would have been shocked by such evaluations of his action at Worms. It was not in the name of individualism that Luther challenged the authority of the church. He saw himself and his conscience as bound or controlled by an external norm: the Scriptures. Luther was even more wary than medieval Catholicism of the ability of the self to determine its own future. The Reformer's words at Worms were bold, but it is hard to draw a direct line from them to modern notions of individual rights and liberties.

It should also be pointed out that while Luther was the leading figure, he was not the only reformer in the early years of the Reformation in Germany. Joining the Wittenberg faculty in 1518 was a young Greek scholar by the name of Philip Melanchthon.

---

24. "Luther at the Diet of Worms, 1521," *WA* 7:838; *LW* 32:112–13.

His skills with biblical languages would prove invaluable as Luther and his followers began to interpret the Scriptures in light of justification by grace through faith. Furthermore, Melanchthon would become a formidable theologian in his own right. In 1521 he authored his own theological textbook, the *Loci Communes* (praised by Luther as worthy of being included in the canon of the Bible!).[25] Melanchthon also wrote the Augsburg Confession (1530), one of the central confessions or faith statements of the Lutheran movement. Also in Luther's circle in the early years were Johann Bugenhagen,[26] who would play a fundamental role in organizing Lutheran churches throughout northern Europe, and Nikolaus von Amsdorf,[27] who was with Luther at the Diet of Worms and introduced the Reformation in several important cities and territories in northern Germany.

As a result of Worms, Luther's excommunication was now official. He was regarded as an outlaw and a heretic by church and state. But his story would take an even more dramatic turn on his way home to Wittenberg. Frederick the Wise, desiring to buy some time for his beleaguered professor, arranged for Luther to be kidnapped and placed in the Wartburg Castle in Eisenach. Nine months later, following a period of internment when he translated the New Testament into German, Luther returned to Wittenberg. Much to his surprise (heretics had not fared well in the hands of the church—witness the case of Jan Hus, burned at the stake in 1415), Luther lived another twenty-five years. In addition to getting married and having a family, he used the time to shape and nurture what became known as the Lutheran Reformation.[28]

---

25. Von Loewenich, *Martin Luther*, 204.

26. *ER* I: 226–27.

27. *ER* I: 27–28.

28. This introduction provides an overview of Luther's early life and teaching. The goal is to help the reader understand the historical and theological context of

Hans Brosamer,
Katherine von Bora, 1530,
woodcut. Schlossmuseum, Gotha.

Hans Brosamer,
Martin Luther, 1530, woodcut.
Schlossmuseum, Gotha.

Luther and "Freedom"

Readers of "The Freedom of a Christian" should keep in mind how Luther used the word *freedom*. It is difficult to give a precise definition.[29] Our culture tends to think of freedom in an economic or political sense. In other words, to be free is to have a wide choice of consumer products or to have a range of options

---

"The Freedom of a Christian." But it would be unfortunate if this was taken to mean that the young Luther is the whole Luther. In fact, the vast majority of his writing takes place after 1520. There are many fine treatments of Luther's later years. James Kittelson's *Luther the Reformer: The Story of the Man and His Career* (Minneapolis: Fortress Press, 1986) is a comprehensive and clear account. Mark U. Edwards's *Luther's Last Battles: Politics and Polemics, 1531-46* (Minneapolis: Fortress Press, 2004 [1983]) is a great resource on the controversies Luther faced in the 1530s and 1540s.

29. As Mark U. Edwards points out, even in Luther's day "Christian freedom" was interpreted in a variety of ways. See Mark U. Edwards, "The Reception of Luther's Understanding of Freedom in the Early Modern Period," *Lutherjahrbuch* 62 (1995):104–20.

when visiting a polling booth. Neither of these definitions of freedom should be minimized. After all, closed societies that severely limit consumer choice and restrict political liberty bring to mind the grey, oppressive, and bureaucratic regimes that ruled in Eastern Europe prior to the fall of the Berlin wall in 1989. Few would point to these states as just ways to organize human communities. But these economic and political definitions of freedom do not really address Luther's concerns.

Further complicating the task of understanding Luther's view of freedom is our historical location on this side of the eighteenth-century Enlightenment. This movement tended to define freedom as deliverance from oppressive thought structures, especially those connected with church dogma. The goal was to be "autonomous," not ruled by any external laws or norms, especially those of the ecclesiastical establishment. As a result, "self-rule" became closely associated with freedom. Again, there is much to be valued in this understanding of freedom. The church did restrict thought in ways that often served the interests of the few. It sometimes created a suffocating intellectual climate in the name of protecting the Bible or the church. But this is yet another definition of freedom that is far from Luther's view. He would have been puzzled by the Enlightenment's belief in autonomy.

Luther was convinced that the self simply lacked the resources to govern itself in a way that would lead to true liberation. As he made clear in "The Freedom of a Christian," the picture of humanity that emerges in light of God's laws and commandments is anything but a self under control. Instead, human beings are driven and frightened, knowing despair and pride much more than an autonomy that claims to be both "master of fate" and "captain of the soul."[30] Rather than knowing real

---

30. See the poem "Invictus" by William Ernest Henly in *Leading Lives That Matter*, Mark R. Schwehn and Dorothy Bass, eds. (Grand Rapids: Eerdmans, 2006), 434–35.

freedom, people are much more prone to cling to some earthly good such as wealth, status, or sex. The result can be a bondage that is deep and profound. And it often is ironic because it can happen under the guise of a supposedly autonomous self that is simply doing as it pleases.

The "freedom" Luther has in mind is deeply relational. As he makes clear in "The Freedom of a Christian," it is found in a relationship with Christ, who has liberated the self from a horizon limited by the forces of "sin, death, and the devil" mentioned at the beginning of this introduction. Parallels in the human realm are difficult to locate. Perhaps analogies can be seen in long-term relationships that have an abundance of faith and trust, such as a faithful marriage or good friendship that has known much joy and sorrow. Within such relationships there is little pretension or need to prove one's worth or value. Hours can pass without a word, and yet there is no need to explain the silence. This sense of freedom cannot be purchased on the market or obtained via a ballot box. It cannot be generated through the earnest efforts of an individual will. Rather, it is a gift of the relationship itself.

Furthermore, as Luther makes clear, for the one on whom this freedom is conferred, the world now becomes an arena for service and good works. The bondage formerly known in relation to "sin, death, and the devil" is transferred now to the needs of the neighbor and the world, but the motivation is completely transformed. The very love that has enabled freedom now flows forth in service.[31] It is not timid or sentimental; the shape of this love itself is cruciform. Consequently, those held by this love should not be surprised to find themselves in the midst of a remarkable adventure that reflects both the suffering and joy of Christ's death and resurrection. As Luther says in "The Freedom of a Christian": "From faith there flows a love and joy in the

---

31. A classic study in Luther's ethics is George Forell's *Faith Active in Love* (New York: American, 1954).

Lord. From love there proceeds a joyful, willing, and free mind that serves the neighbor and takes no account of gratitude or ingratitude, praise or blame, gain or loss. We do not serve others with an eye toward making them obligated to us. Nor do we distinguish between friends and enemies or anticipate their thankfulness or ingratitude. Rather we freely and willingly spend ourselves and all that we have. . . . "[32]

The Texts

The translation of Luther's Letter to Pope Leo X is based on the Latin text found in *WA* 7:42–49. Also used in the preparation of the text was the English translation by W. A. Lambert (rev. Harold J. Grimm) as found in *LW* 31:334–343 and the German translation by Fidel Rädle in *Martin Luther: Lateinisch-Deutsche Studienausgabe*.[33]

The translation of "The Freedom of a Christian" is based on the Latin text as found in *WA* 7:49–73. Also acknowledged is the assistance of the English translation by W. A. Lambert (rev. Harold J. Grimm) as found in *LW* 31:343–377 and the German translation by Fidel Rädle in *Martin Luther: Lateinisch-Deutsche Studienausgabe*.[34]

---

32. "The Freedom of a Christian, 1520." See my translation on page 83.

33. Johannes Schilling, ed. (Leipzig: Evangelische Verlagsanstalt, 2006), II:101–19.

34. Ibid., 120–85.

MARTIN LUTHER'S

LETTER TO
POPE LEO X

1520

JESUS

To Leo X, the Pope in Rome, Martin Luther sends his greetings in Christ Jesus our Lord. Amen.

Living among the monsters of this age, with whom I have battled for the last three years, I am compelled at times to look to you and to think of you, Leo, most blessed father. Indeed, since you are regarded as the sole cause of my struggles it is almost impossible for me not to think of you. You should know that the godless and faithless flatterers surrounding you have led me to appeal from your see to a future council.[1] I do this in spite of the empty decrees of your predecessors, Pius and Julius, who acted like tyrants and foolishly denied this course of action.[2] I would like you to know that in my heart I continue to wish you and your see the very best and I seek God's blessing for you in earnest prayer. Now I fully admit that I have despised and dismissed those who have attempted to frighten me with the power of your name and authority; however, there is one item that I cannot ignore and it is the reason I am writing to you,

---

1. Luther's letter to Leo presumes a familiarity with the structure of the Roman Catholic hierarchy and its recent history. The pope was surrounded by a court of councilors known as the curia. This included the college of cardinals, who were bishops that advised the pope and who also had the power to elect a new pope in the event of a vacancy. In the late Middle Ages the office of the pope suffered a tremendous loss of authority, primarily as a result of greed and political intrigue. Consequently, a movement known as "conciliarism" gained momentum in the church. It asserted that a council of bishops, under certain circumstances, had the power to offset the influence of the pope and address abuses that were being ignored. There were numerous calls for a council to deal with the crisis in the church in the early sixteenth century. The Council of Trent finally met from 1545–1563.

2. Luther is referring to Leo's immediate predecessors, Pope Pius III (1503) and Pope Julius II (1503–1513). Both saw a council as a challenge to their authority.

Holy Father. It is said that I am guilty of a great mistake because I have attacked you personally.

However, I truly wish you to know that, by my understanding, I have said only the best things regarding you. If I have ever done otherwise, it should not be condoned. Indeed, I would agree with the judgment of my opponents and take back my words. I have called you a "Daniel in Babylon"[3] and anyone with the ability to read knows that I defended your innocence against Sylvester,[4] who called your integrity into question. Your reputation and the fame of your blameless life are celebrated throughout the world in the writings of many great figures and are too well known to be questioned by anyone. I am not so foolish to attack someone whom all people praise. I will always strive to avoid attacking anyone who falls from public favor. I take no pleasure in the faults of others since I am very aware of the beam in my own eye (Matt. 7:3). Also, I would not be the first one to cast a stone at the woman caught in adultery (John 8:1-11).

Now I will admit to attacking false or unchristian teachings. I have not criticized the bad morals of my opponents but rather their ungodly doctrines. I am not going to repent of this! After all, I am only following the example of Christ, who did not hesitate to call his opponents such things as "a brood of vipers," "blind fools," "hypocrites," and "children of the devil" (Matt. 23:13, 17, 33; John 8:44). And Paul accused Elymas the magician (Magus) of being a "son of the devil . . . full of all deceit and

---

3. A reference to Daniel in the Old Testament, who refused to stop worshiping God while in captivity in Babylon. See Daniel 6:1-28.

4. Sylvester Mazzolini (1456–1523), also known as Prierias, was a Dominican theologian with a very strong view of the pope's authority. He defended the selling of indulgences because they were authorized by the pope, who spoke without error (infallibly) about faith and morals. Luther believed this view was actually an insult to the pope because it exalted him over the Scriptures. See Martin Brecht, *Martin Luther: His Road to Reformation 1483–1521*, trans. James L. Schaaf (Philadelphia: Fortress Press, 1985), 242–46.

villainy" (Acts 13:10), and he labels others as "dogs," "deceivers," and "adulterers" (Phil. 3:2; 2 Cor. 11:13). When judged by the standards of a sensitive audience, who is more biting and unrestrained in his comments than the Apostle Paul (2 Cor. 2:17)? And think of the stinging criticism of the prophets! However, our ears have become more finely tuned to the empty praises of the endless lines of flatterers. As a result, we protest when any of our opinions meets with disapproval. If we are unable to avoid the truth in any other way, we attack the methods of our opponents, saying they are too aggressive, impatient, and arrogant. But what is the use of salt if it does not bite? What use is the sword if it does not cut? As Jeremiah says, "Accursed is the one who is slack in doing the work of the Lord" (Jer. 48:10). Therefore, blessed Leo, when you read this letter and understand my intentions, I hope you see that I have never meant ill toward you personally.[5] I have only the best wishes for you. I have no argument with any person with regard to morals. But I am unyielding when it comes to contending about the word of truth. In all other things, I gladly will yield, but I have neither the power nor the will to deny the word. If others view my motives differently, they either are not thinking straight or have failed to understand what I have said.

However, the situation of the Roman curia—which neither you nor anyone else can deny—is more disastrous than that of Babylon or Sodom. As far as I am able to determine, it is totally

---

5. See Berndt Hamm, "Luther's 'Freedom of a Christian' and the Pope," *Lutheran Quarterly* 21, no. 3 (Autumn 2007): 249–67. Hamm makes a strong case that Luther's letter to Leo X and his treatise, "The Freedom of a Christian," mutually interpret each other. Luther is biting in his criticism of those who teach falsely because they bind consciences and suffocate Christian freedom; however, he is also committed to loving his neighbor, even if he or she is an "enemy." Therefore, this letter should be seen as an attempt to practice the principles put forth in the treatise. Luther shows genuine concern about Leo as a person while being unsparing in his attack of any theological position that threatens Christian liberty.

depraved, hopeless, and unrestrained in its godlessness. I have also been angry at the way good Christians have been mocked in your name and under the cover of the Roman church. I have resisted and will continue to resist your see as long as the spirit of faith lives in me. I am realistic about this. I know that by my efforts alone nothing will fundamentally change in that chaotic Babylon. I recognize that the fury of the flatterers is too intense for me to overcome; however, I do feel an obligation to warn my fellow Christians so that some of them may avoid being harmed by the plague of Rome. At the very least, perhaps the damage can be limited.

As you know, for many years the world has been flooded— indeed the entire globe has been inundated—by this Roman plague that has destroyed bodies, souls, and possessions. What we have on display is the worst example of the worst possible things. It is clear as day to everyone that the Roman church, once the most holy of all, has become a den of robbers (Matt. 21:13), the most shameless of brothels, and the kingdom of sin, death, and hell combined. Things are so bad that if the Antichrist himself appeared he could think of nothing to add to its wickedness.[6]

You sit in the midst of this, Leo, like a lamb among wolves (Matt. 10:16). You are like Daniel in the midst of lions (Dan. 6:16). Similar to Ezekiel, you live among scorpions (Ezek. 2:6). Even if you were to call to your side three or four learned and trustworthy cardinals you would not have a chance. All of you would be poisoned before you could develop the means to remedy the situation. It is plain for all to see that the Roman curia is lost. God's eternal wrath has fallen upon it. The curia hates

---

6. The Antichrist is a controversial figure in the Christian tradition. Many saw the Antichrist as the chief opponent of Christ, whose terrible reign marked the end of history. While Luther was ambivalent about the pope and his authority early in his career, by the early 1520s he identified the papacy with the Antichrist. See Scott Hendrix, *Luther and the Papacy: Stages in a Reformation Conflict* (Philadelphia: Fortress Press, 1981).

councils, resists reformation, and is powerless in the face of its own corruption. What was said of its mother Babylon also applies to it: "We tried to heal Babylon, but she could not be healed. (Let us) forsake her . . ." (Jer. 51:9). It was the duty of you and your cardinals to do something about this evil state of affairs, but the disease proved far too pervasive to be remedied by a healing hand. Indeed, neither the chariot nor the horse responds to the rein.[7] Because of my affection for you, Leo, I am deeply saddened that you are the pope in this day and age. The Roman curia does not deserve you or anyone like you. Instead, Satan himself should be the pope, for he is the one who appears to be ruling more than you in this Babylon.

How much better it would be, Leo, if you would abandon the splendor and glory that your enemies claim belongs to your office! You could live on the income of an ordinary parish priest or on your family's inheritance. The only ones who should glory in such extravagance are the sons of Judas, the family of shame and ruin. What, exactly, are you accomplishing in the Roman curia, my Leo? After all, your name is being used by dishonorable and deceitful people to reduce men and women to poverty, destroy souls, increase crime, and suppress faith and truth throughout the church of God. It is true, unhappy Leo, that you sit on a particularly dangerous throne. I speak this truth to you only because I wish you well. If Bernard of Clairvaux[8] had compassion on Pope Eugenius at a time when the Roman see was very corrupt—though with more hope for improvement than is the case today—why shouldn't we complain about our situation?

---

7. A reference to the classical Roman author Virgil. See *Virgil's Georgics*, trans. Janet Lembke (New Haven: Yale University Press, 2005), 20.

8. Bernard of Clairvaux (1090–1153) was a French monk known for his powerful writing and preaching. His book *On Consideration* spoke to Pope Eugenius III about the spiritual temptations that come to someone who serves in a powerful office like the papacy.

After all, during the past three centuries we have witnessed an increase in the amount of corruption and wickedness. Is it not true that under the great span of heavens there is nothing more corrupt, noxious, and offensive than the Roman curia? It even surpasses by any measure the godlessness of the Turks. It once may have been the gate of heaven, but now it is the very mouth of hell, held open by the wrath of God. In light of this situation, there is only one thing to do: call attention to the danger and hope that a few people will be saved from the Roman abyss.

Now you can see, my Father Leo, my intention in my raging against this corrupt see. My fury has not been directed against you personally. Indeed, it was my hope to gain your favor and even save you with a strong and forceful assault against the prison (truly a hell) that surrounds you. For the sake of your own salvation and that of many others, it is important to have talented and able people do all they can to counter the confusion created by this corrupt curia. Those who claim to serve your office actually harm it. They say they are glorifying Christ, but in fact they are cursing him. In short, it is not possible to be a Christian and a Roman.

I want to be even clearer about this. It was never my intention in the beginning to attack the Roman curia or to raise questions about it. However, when I saw that all attempts to remedy the situation were hopeless, I was full of contempt for it and gave it a certificate of divorce (Deut. 24:1), saying, "Let the evildoer still do evil, and the filthy still be filthy" (Rev. 22:11). Then I began a quiet and peaceful study of the holy Scriptures, in order to assist my brothers around me. As I progressed in these studies, Satan opened his eyes and filled his servant, John Eck, a noted enemy of Christ, with an uncontrollable desire for worldly glory.[9] The result was that Eck dragged me unwittingly into a

---

9. John Eck (1486–1543) was a professor at Ingolstadt and long-time opponent of Luther. His opposition to Luther at the Leipzig Debate of 1519 forced Luther

debate and focused on one little word that I let slip concerning the primacy of the Roman church. This Thraso,[10] this conceited bragger, frothing at the mouth and gnashing his teeth, declared that he would risk everything for the glory of God and honor of the apostolic see. Inflated with the idea of abusing your authority, he was confident of his ability to win a victory over me. He was less concerned with defending the primacy of Peter than he was with establishing his own primacy among the theologians of our time. Given this desire, it was important for him to triumph over Luther. When the debate ended unhappily for the sophist, he was gripped by an unbelievable madness. He actually thought he alone was responsible for my disclosure of the shame and wickedness of Rome.

Therefore, most excellent Leo, allow me to make my case and reveal your true enemies. I believe you are aware of the conversations I had with Cardinal St. Sisto, an unwise and unhappy man who is not really to be trusted. Out of regard for your name, I placed myself and my case in his hands; however, he did not try to establish peace—which is something he could have accomplished with one little word. I promised to remain silent and bring an end to the strife, provided my opponents agreed to do the same; however, Cajetan sought his own glory and did not hold up his end of the argument.[11] He began to defend my opponents and gave them freedom to speak. At the same time,

---

to acknowledge that his quarrel with Rome was not primarily about indulgences but about the papacy itself and its claim to be the final judge of biblical truth. See *ER* 2:17–19.

10. Thraso is a vain character in the Roman author Terence's comedy *The Eunuch*.

11. Cardinal Cajetan (1469–1534), also known as Cardinal St. Sisto, was a Dominican theologian who was also an expert in the theology of Thomas Aquinas. As a papal representative, he met with Luther in the city of Augsburg in October of 1518 and called upon the Wittenberg Reformer to recant his teaching on indulgences. See *ER* 1:233–34.

he ordered me to recant, which was not a part of our original agreement. Up to this point, things were going fairly well. But his inconsiderate and arbitrary behavior led to a situation that became far worse. So do not blame Luther for what happened next. The responsibility rests with Cajetan alone. His actions simply did not permit me to remain silent, though at the time it was my desire not to speak. Given this sequence of events, what else could I possibly have done?

Next followed Karl Miltitz, who was also a nuncio of Your Holiness.[12] He traveled extensively, making an earnest attempt to restore the order that Cajetan in his blindness and arrogance had attempted to destroy. Miltitz finally managed, with the help of that most illustrious prince Elector Frederick, to arrange several private conferences with me. Once again I renewed my pledge to be silent, and I even accepted either the archbishop of Trier or the bishop of Naumberg to serve as a referee in the dispute. This appeared to bring the matter to a place where there would be a good prospect for success; however, Eck, that other great enemy of yours, intervened by arranging the debate at Leipzig with Dr. Karlstadt.[13] When the new question about the primacy of the pope was raised, Eck turned his weapons toward me and completely ruined the plans we had made for keeping the peace. Meanwhile, Karl Miltitz waited. Judges were selected and the debate took place; however, no decision regarding the results of the debate was forthcoming. This was hardly surprising given Eck's lies, deceptions, and cunning tricks. Once again, things were stirred up, confused, and muddled worse than ever.

---

12. Karl Miltitz (1490–1529) was a papal nuncio (ambassador) who attempted to mediate the growing dispute between Luther and Rome in 1518 and 1519. See *ER* 3:63.

13. Andreas Bodenstein von Karlstadt (1483–1541) was a colleague of Luther on the Wittenberg faculty who also debated John Eck at the aforementioned Leipzig Debate of 1519. See *ER* 1:178–80.

Matthias Gerung, *Shipwreck of the Catholic Clergy*, 1545, woodcut.

Given these circumstances, a decision was almost beside the point because a huge wildfire was bound to be the end result. It is clear that Eck sought only his own glory and not the truth. Again, there was nothing I failed to do that I otherwise should have done in these circumstances.

I concede that on this occasion much of Rome's corruption came into public view. But the wrong done in this case was the fault of Eck. He simply undertook a task that was beyond his capability. Striving for his own glory, he ended up revealing the shame of Rome to the entire world. This man is your real enemy, my Leo, or rather the enemy of your curia. In fact, we can all learn from his example, namely, that no enemy is more dangerous than a flatterer. What has he accomplished with his flattery other than an evil not even the power of a king might be capable of doing? The name of Rome is nothing but a stench throughout the entire world. Papal authority has seldom been held in lower esteem. And Roman ignorance, once famous, is now despised. We would not have heard anything about these things if Eck had not frustrated the peace process arranged by Karl [Miltitz] and me. He now realizes what has happened and is furious that my books were published. But his outburst is too late and will amount to nothing. He should have thought of this earlier when, like a whinnying horse, he sought only his own glory and believed that he could use you to his own advantage; however, he ended up endangering your authority. This vain man hoped that out of fear for your name I would stop and be silent. He thought this would work, for I do not believe he entirely trusted his own intelligence and learning. Now he recognizes that my courage is greater than he previously realized and that I have not been silent. So now he repents of his rash actions, but it is too late. Finally he understands (if he truly does) that there is one in heaven who opposes the proud and humbles those who are presumptuous (1 Pet. 5:5; James 4:6).

This disputation only resulted in greater confusion regarding the Roman cause. Karl Miltitz, trying for a third time to bring about peace, came to the chapter meeting of the Augustinian brothers. He consulted with them, asking their advice about how to handle this matter that had become both disturbing and dangerous. By God's grace there was no hope of resolving the matter by violent means. As a result, some of the leaders of the Order were sent to me. They requested that I at least honor your

Blessedness as a person and in a humble letter acknowledge that both of us are innocent in this affair. They also said they did not think the situation was hopeless as long as Leo X, out of his goodness, took an active role in the proceedings. I have always desired peace so I could devote myself to quieter and more useful studies. The anger and fury I have exhibited—by loud and violent words and by means of my intellect—are merely for the purpose of overwhelming my opponents. But when I heard the suggestion of these leaders, I gladly ceased all my talk. With joy and thanksgiving I welcomed their advice as long as we can see our hopes bear fruit.

So, most Blessed Father, I come bowing low before you, asking you to take this matter into your own hands and rein in these flatterers and enemies of peace (who only pretend to keep the peace). But let no one think, Blessed Father, that I will recant unless he or she wants even more turmoil and trouble. Furthermore, I acknowledge no laws for the interpretation of the word of God, since the word of God teaches freedom in all other matters and must not be bound (2 Tim. 2:9). If these two points are not contested, I would be willing to do or endure most anything. I hate contention and will not challenge anybody; however, I do not want others to provoke me either. If I am provoked, as Christ is my teacher, I will not remain silent. Your Blessedness, with a short and simple word, is able to bring this controversy to an end and command both sides to keep the peace. And this word is what I have always wanted to hear.

Therefore, my Father Leo, do not listen to those sirens that pretend you are not a mere human but some sort of divine being who can command and decide whatever you wish. Things cannot be done this way; you do not have such power. For you are the servant of servants and more than all others you are in a most miserable and dangerous situation. Do not be deceived by those who pretend you are lord of the world or who claim that no one can be a Christian unless he or she accepts your authority. Do not listen to those who claim you have power over heaven, hell, and purgatory. Such people are your enemies and are seeking to destroy your soul. As the prophet Isaiah says: "O my people, they that call thee blessed, the same deceive thee" (Isa. 3:12). They are mistaken when they place you above a council and the universal church. They are also mistaken when they give you alone the right to interpret Scripture. Under the protection of your name, they desire only to promote their unchristian teaching in the church. And unfortunately, through them Satan has made much progress, just as he did under those who preceded you in the papacy.

In summary, do not believe those who exalt you; rather you should believe those who humble you. This is the judgment of God who "has brought down the powerful from their thrones, and lifted up the lowly" (Luke 1:52). Observe the great difference between Christ and his successors, though they all wish to be regarded as his substitute here on earth. I fear that most of them have viewed themselves as Christ's substitute in an all too real a sense! A person is a substitute only when the superior is absent. If the pope rules and at the same time Christ is not present or is not ruling in his heart, then what else is he but a substitute for Christ? What is the church other than an assembly of people without Christ? And it follows—what is such a substitute other than an antichrist or an idol? Were not the apostles much more right in calling themselves the servants of the present Christ rather than the substitutes of an absent Christ?

Perhaps I am presumptuous in attempting to teach one from whom we all ought to learn. After all, as your wicked and self-serving followers boast, the rulers of our day who have the responsibility of judging others in fact receive their decisions from you. But I am following here the example of St. Bernard and his book to Pope Eugenius entitled *On Consideration*.[14] It is a text every pope should know by heart. I do this not because I am eager to instruct you but out of a pure and loyal concern that we ought to have for all of our neighbors. Such concern should have no regard for their status, whether it be high or low, but is rather focused on the advantages and the dangers of each particular situation. I know that Your Blessedness is tossed and driven by many storms in Rome. That is, you are far out at sea and threatened on all sides by danger. You are working hard in these miserable conditions and thus can use a little help from one of the least of your brothers. Therefore I do not consider it foolish to forget your high office in order to do what love demands. I will not play the role of a flatterer in this serious and dangerous situation. If others do not recognize me as a most humble subject and friend, at least I know there is One who understands and judges all things.

In conclusion, to avoid approaching you with empty hands, Blessed Father, I am sending a short essay that I have dedicated to you. I hope you regard it as a sign of peace and good hope. In this treatise you will be able to discern the kind of studies on which I want to spend my time. Such labor would be possible if your godless flatterers permit me the opportunity to do such work. Regarding its size, the book is small; however, unless I am mistaken, it contains a summary of the entire Christian life—provided you grasp its meaning. I am a poor man and have no other gift to offer you. But then you do not need to be enriched by any gift save a spiritual one. May the Lord Jesus preserve you forever. Amen.

Wittenberg, September 6, 1520

---

14. See note 8.

THE FREEDOM
of a
CHRISTIAN

1520

MARTIN LUTHER

Introduction

Many people view the Christian faith as something easy, and some even place it among the virtues.[1] They do this because they have not experienced faith, nor have they tasted its great power. A person must experience the strength faith provides in the midst of trials and misfortune. Otherwise, it is not possible to write well about faith or to understand what has been written about it. But one who has had even a small taste of faith can never write, speak, reflect, or hear enough concerning it. As Christ says, it is a "spring of water welling up to eternal life" (John 4:14).

Although I cannot boast of my own abundance of faith, and I also know quite well how short my own supply is, nevertheless I hope I have attained at least a drop of faith—though I grant that I have been surrounded by great and various temptations.[2]

---

1. Luther is challenging a tradition of medieval theology that listed faith as one of the theological virtues along with hope and love. As he will try to demonstrate in "The Freedom of a Christian," faith alone is sufficient—it does not need hope and love to "complete" it. For Luther faith or trust (see also note 7) was the fundamental perspective for all of life. It involves not only intellectual assent but an orientation of the whole self. For example, when discussing the first commandment ("You are to have no other gods"), Luther provides the following explanation for how "god" is to be understood: "A god is the term for that to which we are to look for all good and in which we are to find refuge in all need. Therefore, to have a god is nothing else than to trust and believe in that one with your whole heart." Martin Luther, The Large Catechism, in *BC*:386.

2. Luther may be referring here to his experience in the monastery, when he wrestled with God and his sense of unworthiness. Later in life he reflected on this period: "I tried to live according to the (monastic) rule and I used to be contrite, to confess and enumerate my sins; I often repeated my confession and zealously performed my required penance. And yet my conscience would never give me assurance, but I was always doubting and said, 'You did not perform that correctly. You were not contrite enough. You left that out of your confession.'" "Lectures on Galatians, 1535," *WA* 40(2):15, *LW* 27:13. Luther's whole life was

However, I hope that in what follows I am able to discuss faith in a way that is more elegant, and certainly with more clarity, than has been done in the past by the literalists and subtle disputants, who have not even understood what they have written.[3]

In order to make the way smoother for the average or common readers (for only them do I serve), I will put forth two themes concerning the freedom and bondage of the spirit.

A Christian is lord of all, completely free of everything.[4]

A Christian is a servant, completely attentive to the needs of all.

These two assertions appear to conflict with one another; however, if they can be found to be in agreement, it would serve our purposes beautifully. Both are statements from the Apostle Paul. He says in 1 Corinthians 9:19: "For though I am free with respect to all, I have made myself a slave to all." And in Romans 13:8 he asserts: "Owe no one anything except to love one another." It is in the very nature of love to be attentive to others and to serve the one who is loved. So it is the case with Christ. Although he was Lord of all and "born of woman, born under the law" (Gal. 4:4), he was at the same time a free man and servant, in "the form of God" and in the "form of a slave" (Phil. 2:6-7).

---

marked by a struggle for faith. This did not disappear when he grasped the meaning of justification by faith.

3. Luther is echoing the complaints of many people in his day (see Erasmus's *The Praise of Folly*) who felt that much theological teaching was hopelessly tangled in the discussion of irrelevant questions, thereby neglecting what was really important.

4. Harold Grimm (*LW* 31:344) translates the Latin *nulli subiectus* as "subject to none"; however, this fails to comprehend Luther's concern in this essay that *all* relationships (including inanimate things like money, property, and diet) are encompassed by Christian freedom.

The Human Being as Inner and Outer Person

THE INNER PERSON

In order to explain this more clearly, let us begin with an example that will eventually lead us to the topic. In every person there are two natures—one that is of the spirit and one that is of the body. When speaking of the spiritual nature or the soul, we are referring to that which is "inner" or "new."[5] When speaking of the bodily nature, or that which is flesh and blood, we are referring to that which is called "sensual," "outward," or "old." Paul writes in 2 Corinthians 4:16: "Even though our outer nature is wasting away, our inner nature is being renewed day by day." Given this difference of natures, it is not surprising that they come into conflict with one another. As the Bible notes, these two natures contend against each other like two persons struggling against each other in the same body. This is what Paul means in Galatians 5:17: "For what the flesh desires is opposed to the Spirit, and what the Spirit desires is opposed to the flesh."

Let us begin by looking inside ourselves at the righteous, free, and true Christian, that is, the spiritual, new, and inner person, and observe how the transformation to this state occurs. It is evident that nothing external can produce Christian righteousness or freedom. Nor can anything external produce unrighteousness or servitude. This can be proven by a simple argument. How is the soul able to benefit if the body is in good health—free, active, and in general eating and drinking and doing what it pleases? Is it not the case that even the most godless slaves of wickedness can enjoy such pleasures? On the other hand, how

---

5. Care needs to be taken so that Luther's use of "spirit" or "soul" is not confused with other views. Luther did not view the spiritual nature or soul as an independent entity that is somehow separate from the body or, as in some cases, regarded as divine. Luther has a comprehensive view of the Fall: body, mind, and soul all are in rebellion against their Creator. The inner nature is capable of being changed, but it is not in itself something godly or righteous.

will poor health or captivity or hunger or thirst or any other external misfortune harm the soul? Even the most godly people and those with the purest consciences are afflicted with such things. None of this touches upon the freedom or servitude of the soul. Therefore, it does not help the soul if the body wears the sacred robe of a priest or visits holy places or performs sacred duties or prays, fasts, and refrains from certain types of foods.[6] The soul receives no help from any work connected with the body. Such activity does not lead to freedom and righteousness for the soul. The works just mentioned could have been done by any wicked person and produce nothing but hypocrites. Of course, the opposite is also true. The soul is not harmed if the body wears secular or regular clothes, lives in ordinary places, eats and drinks like everyone else, does not pray out loud, and fails to do the things spoken of above that hypocrites can do.

Furthermore, the solution is not to be found in rejecting every kind of work the soul is capable of doing, such as contemplation and meditation. This would result in nothing. One thing and one thing alone leads to Christian life, righteousness, and freedom. This is the holy word of God, the gospel of Christ, as Jesus himself says in John 11:25: "So if the Son makes you free you will be free indeed." And he says in Matthew 4:4: "One does not live by bread alone but by every word that comes from the mouth of God."[7]

---

6. It is hard for the modern reader to appreciate the effort made by late medieval people to secure their salvation. For example, before the Reformation took hold, the Castle Church in Luther's own Wittenberg was famous for its collection of relics—including outlandish items like milk from the Virgin Mary and wood from the crib of the infant Jesus. Those who made a visit to Wittenberg and viewed these relics (and made the appropriate contribution) reduced the time they would serve in purgatory.

7. For Luther the word of God is not simply the Bible. The word is also far more than a source of information. He sees the word as powerful and creative, similar to Genesis 1 in which the world comes into existence through God's speech. Finally, the word refers to Christ (who is understood as the Word of God) and

The One Thing Needed: The Word of God

Let us then consider it certain and firmly established that the soul needs only one thing: the word of God. When this is missing, the soul lacks the one item that is essential. Having the word of God makes the soul rich—for what else could it possibly need? The word of God brings life, truth, light, peace, righteousness, salvation, joy, liberty, wisdom, power, grace, glory, and every other blessing imaginable. This is why in Psalm 119 and in many other places in the Bible there is a yearning and sighing for the word of God. This also makes clear why there is no greater disaster than when God's wrath results in a famine when his word is not heard (for example, see Amos 8:11). Similarly, there is no greater mercy than when God sends his word as in Psalm 107:20: "He sent out his word and healed them, and delivered them from destruction." Thus Christ was given to the world for no other ministry than the word. Similarly, all the apostles, bishops, and priests have been called and instituted only for the ministry of the word.

You may ask, "What is the word of God and how should it be used, since there are so many words of God?" I respond by quoting what Paul says in Romans 1. The word is the gospel of God concerning his son, who was made flesh, suffered, rose from the dead, and was glorified through the Spirit who makes us holy. To preach Christ means to feed the soul, make it righteous, set it free, and save it, provided the preaching is believed. For faith alone is the saving and efficacious use of the word of God. The apostle Paul in Romans 10:9 writes: "If you confess with your lips that Jesus is Lord and believe in your heart that God raised him from the dead, you will be saved." Paul also says in Romans 10:4: "For Christ is the end of the law so that there may be righteousness for everyone who believes." Also, in Romans 1:17

---

the preaching of Christ's death and resurrection in a manner that creates faith in listeners.

it states: "The one who is righteous shall live by faith." The word
of God cannot be received or honored by any works but must be
grasped by faith alone. Therefore, it is clear that the soul needs
only the word of God for life and righteousness; it is justified
by faith alone and not by any works. If the soul were able to be
justified by any other means it would not need the word of God,
and then it also would not need faith. It should be underlined
that this faith cannot exist in connection with works.[8] In other
words, if you hold this faith and at the same time claim to be
justified by works, whatever their character, you are missing the
point. This would be like "limping with two different opinions"
(1 Kings 18:21), or it would be like worshiping Baal and kiss-
ing one's own hand (Job 31:27-28), which, as Job says, is a great
iniquity. Therefore, when you begin to trust,[9] you discover at the
same time that all things in you are wholly blameworthy, sinful,
and deserving of condemnation, as Paul says in Romans 3:23:
"All have sinned and fall short of the glory of God."[10] He also

---

8. In making this claim, Luther is swimming against the stream of the entire
medieval tradition. In the late Middle Ages there were basically two options with
regard to salvation: the teachings of Thomas Aquinas and William of Ockham.
In simplified form, Aquinas taught that the divine gift of faith needed to be
completed by works of love. God's grace made these works possible, but it was
necessary for the human will to cooperate freely with grace in the performance of
works. Ultimately, faith was "empty" until filled by love. Ockham put a greater
stress on human involvement in the process of salvation. He said that we had "to
do what was in us" (*facere quod in se est*) in order to qualify for grace in the first
place. Further, our free wills then had to cooperate with grace to do the works
necessary to be justified. Luther is saying that faith *alone* makes us right with
God.

9. Translation of the Latin *credere*. It can be translated "to believe" or "to trust."
Both translations are used throughout the text, depending upon the context.
Luther did not see faith as merely an act of the intellect. Faith encompassed
the whole being of the person, including the heart. Therefore, "trust," because it
includes other faculties besides the mind, is often preferred over "belief."

10. This subtle point is easily misunderstood. Luther is not saying we have to
run ourselves into the ground and then out of desperation look to God. Rather,

states in Romans 3:10-12: "There is no one who is righteous, not even one . . . all have turned aside, together they have become worthless." When you grasp this, you will know the necessity of Christ, who suffered and rose again for you. Believing in him, you become a new person—one whose sins are forgiven and one who is justified by the merits of another, namely Christ alone.

It is only possible for this faith to rule in the inner person as Paul says in Romans 10:10: "For one believes with the heart and so is justified." Since we are justified by faith alone, it is clear that the inner person cannot be justified, freed, or saved by any external work or act, and such works, whatever they may be, have nothing to do with the inner person. Therefore, only ungodliness and unbelief of the heart make a person a condemned servant of sin—this cannot be caused by any external work or act of sin. It follows that it ought to be the primary goal of every Christian to put aside confidence in works and grow stronger in the belief that we are saved by faith alone. Through this faith the Christian should increase in knowledge not of works but of Christ Jesus and the benefits of his death and resurrection. This is what Peter teaches in the fifth chapter of his first letter (1 Pet. 5:10). No other work makes a Christian. Thus, when the Jews asked Christ in John 6:28 what they must do to perform the works of God, he dismissed their multitude of activities and pointed to one work, saying "This is the work of God, that you believe in him whom he has sent" (John 6:29), for "it is on him that God the Father has set his seal" (John 6:27).

Therefore, true faith in Christ is an incomparable treasure that brings a person complete salvation and deliverance from all evil, as Jesus says in Mark 16:16: "The one who believes and is baptized will be saved; but the one who does not believe will be condemned." The prophet Isaiah contemplated this treasure

---

the birth of God's grace makes you aware that you are completely undeserving of this gift.

Hans Baldung Grier, *Martin Luther with a Nimbus and Dove,*
1521, woodcut.

and foretold it: "The Lord will make a small and consuming
word upon the land and it will overflow with righteousness" (Isa.
10:22).[11] It is as if Isaiah said, "Faith, which is a small but perfect fulfillment of the law, will fill believers with such complete

---

11. It is uncertain what version of the Bible Luther was using here. The Vulgate
(the Latin translation of the Bible used in the medieval period) does not corre-
spond to this translation. The NRSV says, "For though your people Israel were
like the sand of the sea, only a remnant of them will return. Destruction is de-
creed, overflowing with righteousness."

righteousness that they will need nothing else to be righteous." Or as Paul says in Romans 10:10: "For one believes with the heart and so is justified."

What about the Bible?

You might wonder how faith alone, without the works of the law, can justify and confer so many great benefits when it appears that the Bible commands that we do a multitude of works, laws, and ceremonies.[12] Here is how I handle this question. First, it is crucial to remember what has been said above, namely, that faith alone without works of the law is what justifies, frees, and saves. It should be pointed out that the entire Scripture of God is divided into two parts: commands and promises. The commands teach what is good; however, the good that is taught is not done. The commands show us what we ought to do, but they do not give us the power to do it. Thus the commands function in this way: they teach us to know ourselves. By means of the commandments, we recognize our inability to do the good, and they cause us to despair of our own powers. This explains why they are called the old testament and belong to the old testament.[13] For example, the commandment "You shall not covet"

---

12. Here Luther introduces his hermeneutic, or way of interpreting the Bible. Luther is not a fundamentalist in the sense that he regards every word of Scripture to be of equal value, nor would he see the Bible as simply another great work of human literature. He believes the Bible is a divine book, written by human beings, through which God speaks to us in two basic ways: the voice of the law (which makes demands of us) and the voice of the gospel (which comforts and liberates us).

13. The reader needs to be careful here. Luther is not saying the Old Testament is composed of commands while the New Testament only contains God's promises. In this context Luther equates the phrase "old testament" with any part of the Bible that commands the reader to do something. Conversely, he uses "new testament" for any language that contains God's promises. Consequently, there can be "old testament" in the actual New Testament of the Bible (for example, Jesus' command in Matthew 5:48 that we "should be perfect as our heavenly Father is perfect"). And there can be "new testament" in the actual Old Testament, as is

is a precept that proves all of us are sinners. For none of us can avoid coveting, no matter how hard we might struggle against it. In order to keep the commandment against coveting, we must despair of our own ability and seek elsewhere the power we do not find in ourselves. As the prophet Hosea says: "Destruction is your own, O Israel. Your help is only in me" (Hosea 13:9).[14] And our experience with one commandment is the same as our experience with all of them. For it is not possible for us to keep any of the commandments.

Now, when through the commands we come to recognize our powerlessness and become anxious about how to satisfy the law (which must be fulfilled down to the smallest detail—otherwise a person would be condemned without hope), we are humbled and reduced to nothing in our own eyes. For we now realize that there is nothing in ourselves by which we can be saved or justified. It is at this point that the second part of Scripture comes to our aid, namely, the promises of God. These declare the glory of God, saying: "If you wish to fulfill the law and not covet, as the law demands, then come believe in Christ in whom grace, righteousness, peace, liberty, and all things are promised to you. If you believe, you will have these things, but if you do not believe, you will lack them." That which is impossible for you to achieve by fulfilling all the works of the law, which are great in number but nevertheless useless, is now done easily and quickly through faith. God the Father has made all things depend on faith so that whoever has faith has everything, while the one who lacks faith has nothing. Paul says in Romans 11:32: "For God has imprisoned all in disobedience so that he may be merciful to all." The promises of God give what the

---

the case in Psalm 23:1 when we are told that the Lord is our shepherd, causing us not to want.

14. This is not the NRSV translation but rather a translation of the text as given in the Weimar edition. See *WA* 7:52:34–36.

commands demand, in order that everything might be done by God alone—both the giving of the commands and the fulfillment of them.[15] God alone commands and God alone fulfills. Therefore the promises of God belong to the new testament, indeed, they are the new testament.[16]

The Threefold Power of Faith

A. Faith Frees from the Law. Since these promises of God are holy, true, righteous, free, and peaceful words, full of goodness, the soul that clings to them with a firm faith will find itself not only united with these promises but fully absorbed by them. It will share in the power of the promises and, even more, will be saturated and intoxicated by them. If a touch of Christ healed, how much more will this most tender spiritual touch, this absorbing of the word, communicate to the soul all things that belong to the word. This is the means by which the soul, through faith alone without works, is justified and sanctified by the word of God. This word makes the soul true, peaceful, and free. It fills the soul with every blessing and makes the recipient of this word a child of God. As John 1:12 says: "To all who received him, who believed in his name, he gave the power to become the children of God."

Thus it is easy to understand, given the source of faith's great power, why a good work or all works are not equal to it. A good work is not able to cling to the word of God or thrive in the soul. As we have seen, in the soul it is faith alone and the word of God that rule. For the word imparts its qualities to the soul in the same way as heated iron glows like fire because it has been

---

15. There is an echo here of St. Augustine's *Confessions*, where he says: "And all my hope is nothing if not in your exceeding great mercy. Give what you command and command what you will." See Augustine, *Confessions*, trans. and ed. Philip Burton (New York: Knopf, 2001), X:29.

16. See note 13.

united with the flame. Consequently, it is clear that a Christian has all that is needed in faith and does not require works in order to be justified. And if we have no need of works, we also have no need of the law. It follows further that if we have no need of the law we are freed from the law. As 1 Timothy 1:9 says, "The law is not laid down for the innocent. . . ." This is the liberty of the Christian—in essence it is our faith. This freedom does not lead us to live lazy and wicked lives but makes the law and works unnecessary for righteousness and salvation.

B. Faith Honors God. This is the first result of faith. Let us now look at the second. Faith functions in this way: it honors the one it trusts with the most reverent and highest regard. This is necessarily the case because faith sees the one it trusts as truthful and deserving of this esteem. There is nothing similar to our regard for the truthfulness and righteousness of this one, and we honor it when we place our trust in it. Could we ascribe to a person anything greater than truthfulness and righteousness and perfect goodness? Conversely, could greater contempt be shown to a person than to consider him a liar, wicked, and worthy of suspicion? This is exactly what we do when we do not trust him. So when the soul firmly trusts the promises of God, it regards God as truthful and righteous. Nothing greater than this can be said of God. It is the highest worship of God to ascribe to him truthfulness, righteousness, and whatever other qualities ought to be predicated of a power in whom one trusts. When this is done, the soul consents to God's will. It hallows God's name and allows itself to be treated according to God's good pleasure. The soul clings to God's promises, does not doubt them, and trusts that the one who is true, just, and wise will act in a way so that all will be well.

Is not such a soul obedient to God in all things by this faith? What commandment has not been completely filled by such obedience? What is the fulfillment of the commandments other than obedience in all things? However, such obedience is not accomplished by works but by faith alone. Conversely, what is a greater contempt and rebellion against God than not to trust his promises? Is this not making God a liar or doubting that God is truthful? Or, to put it another way, is this not the same as attributing falsehood and vanity to God while lifting up oneself as truthful? Is not the person who does this denying God and setting himself up as an idol in his own heart? For what could be said of good works done in this state of wickedness, even if they were performed by angels and the apostles themselves? Rightly, then, does God see unbelief as the root of sin instead of anger or lust. Those who imagine they are fulfilling the law by keeping chaste and doing works of mercy—things legally required as civil and human virtues—might not be saved. For their deeds are nevertheless included under the sin of unbelief, and they must either seek mercy or be justly condemned.

However, when God sees that we consider him to be truthful and that by the faith of our heart we give him the honor he is due, then he does us the honor of considering us truthful and righteous on account of our faith. Faith results in truth and righteousness by giving to God what belongs to him. Therefore, God glorifies our righteousness. It is true and just that God is true and just, and to confess that God has these qualities is the same as being truthful and just. As God says in 1 Samuel 2:30: "For those who honor me I will honor, and those who despise me shall be treated with contempt." And in Romans 4:3 Paul states that Abraham's faith "was reckoned to him as righteousness" because by his faith he gave the highest glory to God. In the same way our faith will be reckoned to us as righteousness if we trust God.

C. Faith Unites the Soul with Christ. The third incomparable benefit of faith is that it unites the soul with Christ just as a bride is united with her bridegroom. By this solemn vow,[17] as the Apostle Paul teaches, Christ and the soul become one flesh. And if they are one flesh, there is a true marriage between them— indeed, the most perfect of marriages because human marriages are but a shadow of this one true union. Given the marriage between Christ and the soul, it follows that they hold everything in common, the good as well as the evil. Accordingly, the soul that trusts Christ can boast and glory in him since it regards what he has as its own. And it follows that whatever the soul has Christ claims as his own.

Let us look at this exchange in more detail and we shall be able to see its invaluable benefits. Christ is full of grace, life, and salvation while the soul is full of sins, death, and damnation. Now let faith enter the picture and sins, death, and damnation are Christ's while grace, life, and salvation will be the soul's. For if Christ is a bridegroom he must take upon himself that which are his bride's, and he in turn bestows on her all that is his. If he gives her his body and very self, how shall he not give her all that is his? And if he takes the body of his bride, how shall he not take all that is hers?

The result is a most pleasing picture, not only of communion but of a blessed battle[18] that leads to victory, salvation, and redemption. For Christ is God and man in one person. He has not sinned or died and he is not condemned. Nor can he sin, die, or be condemned. The righteousness, life, and salvation he possesses are unconquerable, for he is eternal and all-powerful; however, by the wedding ring of faith, he shares in the sins, death, and hell of his bride. In fact, he makes them his own

---

17. The Latin word is *sacramento*. As Ephesians 5:32 suggests, this could also be translated as "mystery."

18. The Latin is *belli*.

and acts as if they were his own. It is as if he sinned, suffered, died, and descended into hell in order to overcome them all;[19] however, sin, death, and hell could not swallow him. In fact, they were swallowed by him in a mighty duel or battle. For his righteousness is greater than all sin, his life stronger than death, and his salvation more invincible than hell. Thus the soul that trusts Christ and receives him as its bridegroom through its pledge of faith is free from all sins, secure against death and hell, and given eternal righteousness, life, and salvation. As a result of this wedding, Christ takes to himself a glorious bride "without spot or wrinkle . . . cleansing her with the washing of water by the word" (compare Eph. 5:26-27). In other words, this bride is cleansed by faith in the word that grants life, righteousness, and salvation. This marriage of faith, as the prophet Hosea says (Hosea 2:19), results in righteousness, justice, steadfast love, and mercy.

Who can even begin to appreciate what this royal marriage means? Who can comprehend the riches of this glorious grace? Christ, the rich and divine bridegroom, marries this poor, wicked whore,[20] redeems her from all of her evil, and adorns her with all

---

19. By borrowing the imagery of a marriage, Luther is hearkening back to the book of Song of Solomon in the Old Testament, which likens God's affection for Israel to the powerful attraction of two lovers. He is drawing on a long medieval tradition of interpretation of this text (Bernard of Clairvaux wrote over eighty sermons on the Song of Solomon.) Luther is also making clear that the relationship of faith is not an abstraction. Luther goes to daring lengths to demonstrate that God truly shares in the experience of sin and death. In a later treatise he will even speak of God (and not just Jesus) dying on the cross: "I mean it this way: if it cannot be said that God died for us, but only a man, we are lost . . . For God in his own nature cannot die; but now that God and man are united in one person it is called God's death . . ." "On the Councils and the Church, 1539," *WA* 50:590; *LW* 41:103–104.

20. The image here is arresting. By referring to Christ's bride as a whore (*meretricius*), Luther is underlining not only the depths of the human condition but also the reach of divine love. There is an echo here of the Old Testament prophet Hosea, who describes the nation of Israel as a faithless harlot (Hosea 1:2).

of his goodness. It now is impossible for her sins to destroy her, for they are laid on Christ and swallowed up by him. She has her righteousness in Christ, her husband, which she now can boast is her very own. She can set this righteousness over against all of her sins and, in the face of death and hell, say with confidence: "If I have sinned, nevertheless, the one in whom I trust, my Christ, has not sinned. Through our marriage all that is his is mine and all that is mine is his." Thus says the bride in the Song of Solomon (2:16): "My beloved is mine and I am his." This is also Paul's meaning in 1 Corinthians 15:57: "But thanks be to God who gives us the victory through our Lord Jesus Christ." The "victory" here refers to Christ's triumph over sin and death, as Paul notes in the previous verse (1 Cor. 15:56): "The sting of death is sin and the power of sin is the law."

From this you are able to understand why such an emphasis is placed on faith, which alone fulfills the law and justifies without works. You see that the first commandment, "You shall worship one God," is fulfilled by faith alone. Even if you were nothing but good works from the soles of your shoes to the top of your head, you would not be righteous, worship God, or fulfill the first commandment. For God cannot be worshipped rightly unless you ascribe to God that which he is due: the glory of truthfulness and all goodness; however, this cannot be done by works but only by the faith of the heart. It is not the doing of works but the trusting of God that both glorifies him and acknowledges him to be truthful. Therefore, faith alone is the righteousness of the Christian and is also the fulfilling of the commandments. For the one who fulfills the first commandment easily fulfills the rest of them. Works, being inanimate, are not able to glorify God, although they can, if faith be present, be done to the glory of God. At this point in the argument, however, we are not asking about what kind of works are to be done. Rather, we are asking about the person that does them and how God is glorified by them. Thus we have stressed the faith of the heart that is the source and substance of all our righteousness. It is a blind and dangerous doctrine that teaches that the commandments can be fulfilled by works. The commandments must be fulfilled before any works can be done, and the works proceed from the fulfillment of the commandments, as we shall hear shortly.

A Double Honor: Priesthood and Kingship

Let us look more carefully at this grace that our inner person has in Christ. We must recognize that in the Old Testament God consecrated to himself all the firstborn males. This birthright was highly prized because it conferred a double honor on the recipient: that of priesthood and kingship. The firstborn brother was a priest and lord over all the others and a type[21] of Christ—the true and only firstborn son of God the Father and the Virgin Mary. He is the true king and priest but not by the standards of the flesh. For his kingdom is not of this world (see John 18:36). He reigns in heavenly and spiritual matters and consecrates them—things such as righteousness, truth, wisdom, peace, salvation, etc. This reign is not only a heavenly one. All things on earth and in hell are also under his power. Otherwise, how could he protect and save us from them? But this does not form the basis of his kingdom. Nor does his priesthood consist in the outer splendor of robes and sacred gestures like those of the human priesthood of Aaron and the present-day church; however, his priesthood is a spiritual thing. By means of an invisible office in heaven, he intercedes for us before God. In this position he offers himself as a sacrifice and does all the things that a priest ought to do, which is why Paul compares him to Melchizedek in Hebrews

---

21. Luther is interpreting the Bible at this point in a twofold way—according to its literal and spiritual sense. The former is the actual historical understanding of the passage, while the latter points to Christ.

(chapters 6–7). Not only does he pray and intercede for us but he teaches us inwardly through the living instruction of his Spirit and thus performs the two key roles of a priest. Thus the prayers and preaching of human priests are examples of Christ's activity on our behalf in heaven.

Now, just as Christ by his birthright has obtained these two privileges, so he also imparts and shares them with everyone who believes in him. This follows from the marriage mentioned above whereby whatever the husband owns belongs as well to the wife. Thus all of us who trust in Christ are priests and kings in Christ, as it says in 1 Peter 2:9: "But you are a chosen race, a royal priesthood, a holy nation, God's own people, in order that you may proclaim the mighty acts of him who called you out of darkness into his marvelous light."

The nature of this priesthood and kingship are as follows. First, with regard to kingship, every Christian by faith is exalted above all things. By virtue of the spiritual power provided in faith, a Christian is lord of all things and nothing is able to do him harm. It can even be said that all things are made subject to him and compelled to serve his salvation. As Paul says in Romans 8:38: "We know that all things work together for good for those who love God." He also says in 1 Corinthians 3:21-23: "For all things are yours, whether . . . life or death or the present or the future—all belong to you and you belong to Christ." Now, this does not mean that every Christian is placed over all things and given actual physical power over them. This is a madness that has possessed church people in our day. The point is that this type of power belongs to kings, princes, and other people on earth. We know from our daily life that our experience is like that of other people—we suffer many things and even die. Indeed, the more Christian a person is the more evil, suffering, and death he must endure, as we see from the example of Christ himself, the firstborn, and also in the lives of his followers, the saints.

Now, it should be clear that we are speaking of a spiritual power. It rules while surrounded by enemies and is mighty in the midst of oppression. This is nothing other than the "power made perfect in weakness" (2 Cor. 12:9). It is the foundation for our belief that in all things God works for our salvation (Rom. 8:28). The result is that the cross and death are compelled to serve me and work together for my salvation. This splendid privilege, difficult to grasp, is truly an omnipotent power, a spiritual dominion, in which there is nothing so good and nothing so evil that cannot be made to work for my good, provided I trust [God's promises].[22] In this spiritual realm faith alone is needed, and works mean nothing for me here. I need only to let faith in all its freedom exercise its power and dominion. Indeed, this is the priceless power and freedom of the Christian.

Not only are we the freest of kings but we are also priests forever.[23] This is far better than being kings, for as priests we are worthy to appear before God, to pray for others, and to teach one another divine things. These are the duties of priests, and they cannot be granted to anyone who doesn't believe. Thus Christ has made it possible for us, provided we trust him, to be not only his brothers, heirs, and fellow rulers of his kingdom but also his fellow priests. Therefore, we can come before God boldly in the spirit of faith and cry, "Abba, Father." Praying for one another, we do all things that pertain to the duties and visible works of priests. The person who does not believe, however, is in a situation where nothing works for good. In fact, this person ends up

---

22. The Latin is *credidero*. See note 8. Bracketed addition by translator.

23. Luther's "priesthood of all believers" upset the entire medieval hierarchy. In Luther's day it was thought that people who worked in the church (priests, monks, and nuns) had "callings," or vocations. The vast majority (the laity) occupied a spiritually inferior position as they carried out their various responsibilities in life. Implicit in this view is a denial of justification by faith because it assumes that what we do in life brings us closer to God. Luther's startling announcement that we are all priests elevated the laity and gave them the same spiritual status as those who served in the church. Now everyone has a vocation or calling.

being a servant of all, and things turn out badly for him because he wickedly uses them to his own advantage and not to the glory of God. Such a person is not a priest but a wicked person whose prayer becomes sin and who never comes into the presence of God because God does not hear sinners (John 9:31).

Who, therefore, can comprehend the lofty dignity of the Christian? As a result of this royal power, he is able to rule over all things—death, life, and sin. Through his priestly glory he shares in God's omnipotence because he does the things that God asks and desires. As it says in Psalm 145:19: "He (the Lord) fulfills the desire of all who fear him; he also hears their cry and saves them." A person attains this glory not by works but only by faith alone.

From what has been said, it is clear that a Christian is free from all things and reigns over all. Such a person does not need works in order to be righteous and saved. Faith alone confers all these things in abundance; however, if a person were to be so foolish as to presume that a good work is needed to become righteous, free, saved, and Christian, then faith and all its benefits would be lost instantly. Such folly is well illustrated in the fable of the dog who runs along the stream with a piece of meat in his mouth and, deceived by the reflection of the meat in the water, opens his mouth to snap at it and loses both the meat and the reflection.[24]

At this point you might ask: "If everyone in the church is a priest, then how do those we now call priests differ from the laity?" I respond that an injustice is committed when the words "priest," "cleric," "spiritual," and "ecclesiastic" are transferred from all Christians to those few who have those titles in the church. The holy Scriptures make no distinction among them. It gives the names "minister," "servant," and "steward" to those

---

24. Luther made frequent allusions to classical texts in his writings. Aesop's Fables were one of his favorite sources.

in our day who are proudly called popes, bishops, and lords. According to the ministry of the word this latter group ought to serve others and teach them the faith of Christ and the meaning of Christian freedom. Although it is true that we are all equally priests, we are not all able to minister and teach publicly. Paul writes in 1 Corinthians 4:1: "Think of us this way, as servants of Christ and stewards of God's mysteries."

However, that stewardship has become something entirely different in the church of today. It is preoccupied with displays of power and governs in a tyrannical manner. No foreign or worldly power can even be compared to it. It is as if the laity were something other than Christian people. As a result of this perversion, the knowledge of Christian grace, faith, freedom, and even Christ himself has been wholly lost, only to be replaced by human works or laws. As Lamentations (see Lam. 1) puts it, we have become servants of the vilest possible people on earth, who abuse our misfortune and make it serve their own wicked wills.

To return to the main topic, I believe it now is clear that it is not enough or in any way would suffice as an adequate foundation for how to conduct our lives. Unfortunately, this tends to be the fashion of our best preachers. Even worse would be to say nothing of Christ and to teach instead human laws and the decrees of the fathers. And there are many who preach Christ in order to arouse human sympathy for him or to incite anger against the Jews. These views are childish and foolish nonsense. Rather, Christ ought to be preached with this goal in mind— that we might be moved to faith in him so that he is not just a distant historical figure but actually Christ for you and me.[25] In

---

25. In 1519 Luther wrote a treatise called "A Meditation on Christ's Passion" (*WA* 2:136–42; *LW* 42:7–14), in which he expands on this point in more detail. Luther's concern is to avoid an "historical faith" in which one knows the "facts" of Christ's life but avoids encountering the meaning of Christ for one's own life.

other words, the purpose of preaching is to make what is said about Christ effectual in us. Such faith is born and preserved in us by preaching why Christ came, what he brought and gave to us, and the benefits we obtain when we receive him. This happens when Christian liberty—which he gives to us—is rightly taught and we are told in what way as Christians we are all kings and priests and therefore lords of all. Thus, as mentioned earlier, we can believe with confidence that whatever we have done is pleasing and acceptable in the sight of God.

What person's heart, upon hearing such things, will not rejoice greatly and grow so tender that he will love Christ in a way not possible by the observance of works or laws? Who would have the power to harm or frighten such a heart? If the knowledge of sin or the fear of death disturbs it, this heart is nevertheless ready to hope in the Lord. Nor is it afraid when confronted with evil, nor is it dismayed when facing enemies. This heart trusts that the righteousness of Christ has become its own righteousness and that its sin has been transferred to Christ and swallowed up by his righteousness. As has been noted above, this is a necessary consequence of faith in Christ. So the heart learns to scoff at sin and death and say with the Apostle Paul: "Where, O death, is your victory? Where, O death, is your sting? The sting of death is the sin, and the power of sin is the law. But thanks be to God, who gives us the victory through our Lord Jesus Christ" (1 Cor. 15:55-57). Death is swallowed up not only in the victory of Christ but in our own victory as well. For through faith his victory has become our own and by this faith we also are conquerors.

At this point we conclude the first part of the essay concerning our inner person, that is, our liberty and the source of that liberty, the righteousness of faith. We have shown that neither laws nor good works are needed for this righteousness. Indeed, it is harmful if we believe that justification comes through them.

THE OUTER PERSON

Discipline of the Body and Service to the Neighbor

Now let us turn to the second part, which concerns the outer person. Here we shall respond to all of those who are offended by the word "faith." They dismiss what has been said so far and ask: "If faith does all things and alone is sufficient for righteousness, why are good works commanded? Let us take our ease and do no works and be content with faith." I would answer such a wicked person with an emphatic "No!" This would be true if we were only inner or spiritual persons. But this will not happen until the last day and the resurrection of the dead. For as long as we live in the flesh we only begin to make progress toward that which will be perfected in a future life. This is the reason the Apostle Paul says in Romans 8:23 that we attain in this life only the "first fruits of the Spirit." It is only in the future life that the fullness of the Spirit will be received. Thus, at this point in the essay, it is important to stress what was said at the beginning: A Christian is servant of all and made subject to all. Insofar as a Christian is free, no works are necessary. Insofar as a Christian is a servant, all kinds of works are done. We shall now show how this is possible.

Controlling the Body

As I have said, the inner person, in the spirit, is abundantly and sufficiently justified by faith. It can be said that this person lacks nothing. It is true that this faith and its accompanying riches ought to grow day by day to the end of this life. Nevertheless, a Christian remains in this mortal life on earth. In this realm control must be exercised over the body. Also, relationships with the rest of humanity must be cultivated. This is where works begin. In this earthly realm a person cannot enjoy leisure. Here a person must take care to exercise moderate discipline over the body and subject it to the Spirit by means of fasting, vigils, and labor.[26] The goal is to have the body obey and conform—and not hinder—the inner person and faith. Unless it is held in check, we know it is the nature of the body to undermine faith and the inner person.

The inner person is one with God. By faith he is created in the image of God and he is joyful and glad on account of the benefits of Christ that have been given to him. Therefore, it is his sole desire to serve God joyfully without thought of gain, inspired by a love that is free and unconstrained; however, while attempting to do this, he finds in his own flesh a contrary will that desires to serve the world and seeks its own advantage. The spirit of faith cannot tolerate this, and with a joyful zeal it attempts to put the body under control. Thus St. Paul says in Romans 7:22-23: "For I delight in the law of God in my inmost self, but I see in my members another law at war with the law of my mind, making me captive to the law of sin that dwells in my members." In 1 Corinthians 9:27 he also writes: "But I punish my body and enslave it, so that after proclaiming to others I myself should not be disqualified." And in Galatians 5:24 Paul writes: "And those who belong to Christ Jesus have crucified the flesh with its passions and desires."

It is important to make clear, however, that the person doing these works is not justified before God by them. Faith could not endure such a false opinion, since it knows that it alone is responsible for righteousness before God. We must also understand that these works serve the purpose of disciplining the body and purifying it of evil desires. The focus should be on these desires and the best means of purging them. Since by faith the soul is made pure and enabled to love God, it wants all things—the body in particular—to join it in loving and praising God. Thus we cannot be idle. The needs of the body compel

---

26. This recalls the monastic discipline that Luther would have known well.

us to do many good works in order to bring it under control. Nevertheless, it must always be kept in mind that these works do not justify a person before God. Rather, by yielding wholly to God, one does these works out of a spirit of spontaneous love, seeking nothing other than to serve God and yield to him in all earthly labors.

Every person will need to discern the manner and limits of these bodily disciplines. One ought to fast, watch, and labor to the extent that such activities are needed to harness the body's desires and longings; however, those who presume that they are justified by works pay no attention to the need for self-discipline but see the works themselves as the way to righteousness. They believe that if they do a great number of impressive works all will be well and righteousness will be the result. Sometimes this is pursued with such zeal that they become mentally unstable[27] and their bodies are sapped of all strength. Such disastrous consequences demonstrate that the belief that we are justified and saved by works without faith is extremely foolish and a complete misunderstanding of the Christian faith.

Let us use some analogies to make this clearer. We ought to consider the works of a Christian—who is justified and saved by the free mercy of God—as we would the works of Adam and Eve in paradise as well as those of their children, had they not sinned. We read in Genesis 2:15 that "the Lord God took the man and put him in the Garden of Eden to till and keep it." Now, Adam was created righteous, acceptable, and without sin. He had no need from his labor in the garden to be made righteous and acceptable to God. Rather, the Lord gave Adam work in order to cultivate and protect the garden. This would have been the freest of all works because they were done simply to please God and not to obtain righteousness. Adam was already

---

27. Latin *cerebrum ledentes*.

righteous—something that would have been our birthright as well [if Adam and Eve had not sinned].[28]

The works of the person who trusts God are to be understood in a similar manner. Through faith we are restored to paradise and created anew. We have no need of works in order to be righteous; however, in order to avoid idleness and so that the body might be cared for and disciplined, works are done freely to please God. Since in this life we are not fully recreated, and our faith and love are not yet perfect, works that discipline the body ought to be increased. These works do not result in righteousness but are useful to discipline the body as described above.

Another example involves the duties of a bishop. When he consecrates a church, confirms children, or performs some other duty pertaining to his office, he is not made a bishop because he does these things. Indeed, if he were not already a bishop, none of these works would be valid. They would be seen as foolish and childish, even ludicrous. Likewise, the Christian who is consecrated by faith does good works, but these do not make him holier or more Christian. This is accomplished by faith alone. Indeed, if one were not first a believer and a Christian, all of one's works would be nothing more than wicked and damnable sins.

Thus the following statements are true: "Good works do not make a good person, but a good person does good works. Evil works do not make a person wicked, but a wicked person does evil works."[29] It is always necessary that the substance or essence

---

28. Brackets added.

29. Three years previously, Luther wrote in his "Disputation against Scholastic Theology, 1517" that "we do not become righteous by doing righteous deeds but, having been made righteous, we do righteous deeds" (Thesis 40). He goes on to say that this is in opposition to the Ethics of Aristotle, which he terms "the worst enemy of grace" (Thesis 41). See *WA* 1:226; *LW* 31:12.

of a person be good before there can be any good works and that good works follow and proceed from a person who is already good. Christ says in Matthew 7:18: "A good tree cannot bear bad fruit, nor can a bad tree bear good fruit." It is clear that the fruit does not bear the tree nor does the tree grow on the fruit. In reality the reverse is true: the tree bears the fruit and the fruit grows on the tree. It is necessary that the tree is prior to the fruit. The fruit does not make the tree good or bad but the tree itself is what determines the nature of the fruit. In the same way, a person first must be good or bad before doing a good or bad work. For one's works do not make one good or bad, but it is the essence of the person that determines whether a work is good or bad.

A similar thing can be found among those who build houses. A good or bad house does not make a good or bad builder, but a good or bad builder makes a good or bad house. It is a general rule that the product never makes the worker like itself, but rather it is the worker that makes the product like himself. So it is with the works of human beings. As a person is, whether a believer or unbeliever, so is that person's work. The work is good if done in faith and wicked if done in unbelief. But the reverse is not true. A work does not make the person either a believer or unbeliever. Works do not make a person a believer and they do not make a person righteous; however, faith does make a person a believer and righteous, and faith does good works as well. Since works justify no one and a person must be righteous before doing a good work, it is manifestly clear that faith alone, because of the pure mercy of God as expressed through Christ and his word, sufficiently justifies and saves a person. A Christian has no need of any law in order to be saved, since through faith we are free from every law. Thus all the acts of a Christian are done spontaneously, out of a sense of pure liberty. As Christians we do not seek our own advantage or salvation because we are already fully satisfied and saved by God's grace through faith. Now our only motive is to do that which is pleasing to God.

Furthermore, good works do not justify or save an unbeliever. It is also true that evil works do not make one wicked or worthy of damnation. Rather, it is unbelief that makes the person and the tree bad that then results in evil and damnable works. Thus when a person is good or evil, this is caused not by works but rather the person's faith or unbelief. As it says in Sirach 10:14: "This is the beginning of sin, that a person falls away from God." In other words, this happens when there is a lack of trust in God. It also states in Hebrews 11:6: "For whoever would approach God must believe that he exists . . ." And in Matthew 12:23 Christ says: "Either make the tree good, and its fruit good; or make the tree bad and its fruit bad . . . ," as if to say: "Let the one who wishes to have good fruit begin by planting a good tree." Therefore, let the person who wishes to do good works begin not with the works but with the believing, for this alone makes a person good. For nothing is able to make a person good except faith, and nothing can make a person evil except unbelief.

It is true that, when considered on only a human level, works make a person good or bad. But this sort of judgment of good and evil is an outward or external one, as indicated by the words of Christ in Matthew 7:20: "Thus you will know them by their fruits." All of this remains on the surface, however. Many have been deceived by outward appearances and have proceeded to write and teach about good works and how they justify without even mentioning faith. On they go, deceiving themselves and forever deceiving others. They progress but only to a lower level, the blind leading the blind.[30] Wearying themselves with many works, they never come to true righteousness. Paul speaks of

---

30. The scriptural reference is to Matthew 15:14.

such people in 2 Timothy 3:5-7: "Holding to the outward form of godliness but denying its power . . . who are always being instructed and can never arrive at knowledge of the truth."

Therefore, whoever does not wish to fall into the same error as these blind people must look beyond actions, laws, and teachings about works. One must look away from works and focus rather on the person and ask how one is justified. For the person is justified and saved by faith, not by works or laws but by the word of God (that is, the promise of grace). In this way the glory remains God's alone, who saves us not by deeds of righteousness that we have done but according to his mercy, which was given to us by grace when we trusted God's word.

As a result, it becomes easy to understand whether good works are to be rejected or accepted and to fashion a standard by which teachings about works can be evaluated. If works are understood to be the means by which we attain righteousness, they become an oppressive and perverse Leviathan.[31] For they are done under the false impression that one is justified by them. Works become compulsory with the result that freedom and faith are destroyed. If this understanding is linked to works, they are good no longer but are rather worthy of damnation. Such works are not free. Moreover, they blaspheme[32] the grace of God, since to justify and save belongs to God alone. These works presume to be able to do something they are actually powerless to do. This godless pretense is but the fruit of our own foolishness. The result of this violent intrusion of works is to corrupt and diminish the glory of God's grace. Let it be understood that we do not reject good works. Indeed, good works are cherished

---

31. See Isaiah 27:1 and Revelation 12:9.

32. Luther usually chooses his words carefully. Blasphemy was viewed as the worst possible sin. Luther is saying that using good works to obtain God's favor dishonors God in a profound way, since it indicates a lack of trust that God will keep his word.

and taught by us. We do not condemn them for their own sake but on account of this godless addition to them—namely, that righteousness is to be obtained through them. This makes them appear good on the surface when in reality they are not good. Thus they deceive people and lead to the deception of others. They are like a ravenous wolf in sheep's clothing (Matt. 7:15).

But this Leviathan, or the false view that works justify, is impossible to overcome when there is a lack of genuine faith. It controls those who see works as the cause of holiness unless faith, the destroyer, comes and rules in their hearts. Nature itself is unable to drive out this monster. Indeed, it does not even recognize this beast but rather sees it as a sign of a most holy will. Even more, if one adds the influence of custom, which only serves to confirm this false opinion, as wicked teachers have done, it is easy to see how this perspective on works becomes an incurable evil that seduces and destroys countless numbers of people. Therefore, while it is fine to preach and write about penitence, confession, and satisfaction, our teaching is undoubtedly deceptive and diabolical if we do not teach about faith as well. Christ, like John the Baptist before him, not only said "Repent" (Matt. 4:17), but also added the word of faith, saying: "The kingdom of heaven has come near."

We ought to preach not only one of these words of God but both. Out of our treasure comes the old and the new—the voice of the law as well as the word of grace. The voice of the law ought to be made known so that all might fear and know their sins with the ultimate goal being repentance and betterment of life. But our preaching does not stop with the law. That would lead to wounding without binding up, striking down and not healing, killing and not making alive, driving down to hell and not bringing back up, humbling and not exalting. Therefore, we must also preach grace and the promise of forgiveness—this is the means by which faith is awakened and properly taught.

Without this word of grace, the law, contrition, penitence, and everything else are done and taught in vain.

Preachers of repentance and grace still can be found in our time, but they do not explain God's law and promise in a way that a person might learn the source of repentance and grace. Repentance proceeds from the law of God, but faith or grace come from the promise of God. Paul says in Romans 10:17: "So faith comes from what is heard, and what is heard comes through the word of Christ." A person is consoled and exalted by faith in the divine promise after being humbled and led to self-knowledge by threats and fear of the divine law. In Psalm 30:5 it says: "Weeping may linger for the night, but joy comes with the morning."

Service to the Neighbor

This concludes the section of teaching concerning both works in general and those works which a Christian does for himself. Finally, we shall deal with those things that pertain to the neighbor. For we do not live in this mortal body and focus only on it. Rather, we live with all other people on earth. Indeed, we live for others and for ourselves. The reason we discipline our bodies is to serve our neighbors genuinely and freely. In Romans 14:7-8 Paul says: "We do not live to ourselves. If we live, we live to the Lord, and if we die we die to the Lord." In this life we never can be idle and without works toward the neighbor. Rather, it is necessary to live fully among people, conversing and dealing with them as Christ did, who was made in human likeness (Bar. 3:37).[33]

Let us be clear that no one needs to do these things to attain righteousness and salvation. Therefore, we should be guided in all our works by this one thought alone—that we may serve and

---

33. Many church fathers saw this passage as an allusion to the incarnation.

Albrecht Dürer, *Katho's son redeems an evil doer from execution,*
1493, woodcut.

benefit others in everything that is done, having nothing else
before our eyes except the need and advantage of the neighbor.
The Apostle Paul wants us to work with our hands in order to
share with the needy (Eph. 5:28). Notice that he could have said
that we should work to support ourselves. But Paul says that we
work to give to those in need. This is why caring for our body
is also a Christian work. If the body is healthy and fit, we are
able to work and save money that can be used to help those in
need. In this way, the stronger member of the body can serve the
weaker. This demonstrates that we are children of God, caring
and working for the well-being of others and fulfilling the law
of Christ by bearing one another's burdens. Here you have the
true Christian life, one where faith is active in love (Gal. 5:6).

It expresses itself joyfully and lovingly and results in the freest possible service. Satisfied with our own abundance of faith, we Christians serve the neighbor without any hope of reward.

This is similar to what Paul teaches the Philippians. After telling them of the riches they enjoyed through their faith in Christ, he then instructs them in the following way: "If then there is any encouragement in Christ, any consolation from love, any sharing in the Spirit, any compassion and sympathy, make my joy complete: be of the same mind, having the same love, being in full accord and of one mind. Do nothing from selfish ambition or conceit but in humility regard others as better than yourselves. Let each of you look not to your own interests but to the interests of others" (Eph 2:1-4). Here we see clearly the model Paul has in mind for the Christian life. All our works are to be directed toward the benefit of others. Given the abundance of our faith, our life and works become a surplus to be used freely in service of the neighbor.

The Apostle Paul points to Christ as an example of such a life: "Let the same mind be in you that was in Christ Jesus, who, though he was in the form of God, did not regard equality with God as something to be exploited, but emptied himself, taking the form of a slave, being born in human likeness. And being found in human form, he humbled himself and became obedient to the point of death . . ." (Phil. 2:5-8). These rich and life-giving words of Paul have been obscured by those who have not understood the phrases "form of God," "form of a slave," "human form," "human likeness." They have foolishly applied them to the divine and human natures of Christ. However, Paul means this: Although Christ possessed the fullness of God and abounded in all good things—thus needing no works or suffering in order to be righteous or saved (for he had all of this from eternity)—nevertheless, he was not puffed up, nor did he elevate himself above us and assume power over us. This would have been perfectly within Christ's rights, but he chose a contrary way. He lived, worked, suffered, and died just like the rest of humanity. It was as if he had need of all these things and did not have the form of God. But he did all this for our sake in order to serve us. All the things he accomplished in the form of a servant would also become our own.

In the same way that Christ, his head, was rich and full through faith, so a Christian ought to be content with this form of God obtained by faith. And as said earlier, this faith should be increased until it is made perfect. For this faith is life, righteousness, and salvation. It saves and makes one acceptable. It gives the Christian all things that Christ has and confirms what Paul says in Galatians 2:20: "And the life I now live in the flesh I live by faith in the Son of God." Although we Christians are free from all works, we ought to use this liberty to empty ourselves, take on the form of servants, take on human form, and become human in order to serve and help our neighbors in every possible way. This is the very manner in which God in Christ acted and continues to act toward us. And this service to the neighbor ought to be done freely, having regard for nothing except the approval of God. As a consequence the Christian thinks in the following way: "Although I am an unworthy and condemned person, my God has given me in Christ all the riches of righteousness and salvation without any merit on my part. God has done this in an act of free and pure mercy so that I now need nothing except faith that trusts that it is true. Given such a Father—who overwhelms me with riches beyond number—why should I not freely, joyfully, with all my heart and an eager will, do things that I know are pleasing and acceptable to him? I will therefore give myself as a Christ to my neighbor, just as Christ offered himself to me. I will do nothing in this life except what is profitable, necessary, and life-giving for my neighbor, since through faith I have an abundance of all good things in Christ."

From faith there flows a love and joy in the Lord. From love there proceeds a joyful, willing, and free mind[34] that serves the neighbor and takes no account of gratitude or ingratitude, praise or blame, gain or loss. We do not serve others with an eye toward making them obligated to us. Nor do we distinguish between friends and enemies or anticipate their thankfulness or ingratitude. Rather, we freely and willingly spend ourselves and all that we have, whether we squander it on the ungrateful or give it to the deserving. This is just as our Father does, who gives all things to all people richly and freely, making "his sun to rise on the evil and on the good" (Matt. 5:45). As sons and daughters of such a Father, we will act in a similar way. Knowing nothing except this sense of spontaneous joy, by which we do and suffer all things, we are led through Christ to delight in God, who lavishly dispenses all these gifts to us.

Therefore, if we recognize these great and precious things that are given to us (as Paul says in Romans 5:5), our hearts will be filled by the Holy Spirit with a love that makes us free, joyful, and all-powerful. We are able to prevail in time of tribulation, serve our neighbors, and yet be lords of all. There are those who do not recognize the gifts given to them through Christ. For them Christ's birth[35] has no real purpose or meaning. The result is that such people know nothing other than their works and are prevented from tasting and sensing [the gifts of faith].[36] As our neighbor is in need and lacks the things that make us rich in faith, it is important to keep in mind that we, too, were in need and lacked God's mercy. But, freely in Christ, our heavenly Father has come to our aid. So our works ought to be directed

---

34. Latin *animus*.

35. Latin *natus*. For Luther the real significance of Christ is the way his birth, death, and resurrection lead to the salvation of humanity. His exemplary life is important but secondary.

36. Brackets added by translator.

freely toward our neighbor. Each of us should become a Christ to the other. And as we are Christs to one another, the result is that Christ fills us all and we become a truly Christian community.

Who then can even begin to comprehend the glory and riches of the Christian life? It can do all things and has all things and lacks nothing. It rules over sin, death, and hell and at the same time seeks to serve and benefit all people. Unfortunately, this type of life is unknown in our day. It is not preached about or sought after. Indeed, we are totally ignorant of our name and do not even know why we are Christians or bear that name. Now we ought to know that we are named after Christ—and not because he is absent but precisely because he dwells in our midst! Our trust in him means that we are Christs to one another and act toward our neighbors as Christ has acted toward us. But in our time a very human way of teaching sets the tone, telling us that the life of faith involves the seeking of merits and rewards. The result is that Christ is seen simply as a taskmaster who is far harsher than Moses.

We have an excellent example of faith in the virgin Mary.[37] In Luke 2:22 it is written that she submitted to the law of Moses and was purified according to the custom of all women. Note that she was not bound to that law and did not need to be purified. But Mary placed herself under the law freely and willingly, acting just as other women would, so that she does not cause offense or create a scandal. She was not justified by this work, but as one already just she did it freely and willingly. This should be a model for how we think about our works. We do not do them

---

37. Some are surprised that Luther values Mary so highly; however, he sees her as a supreme example of one who trusted God as illustrated by her response to the angel Gabriel's announcement that she would bear God's Son: "Here am I a servant of the Lord; let it be with me according to your word" (Luke 1:38). His "Commentary on the Magnificat, 1521" was completed shortly after "The Freedom of a Christian." See *WA* 7:538–604; *LW* 21:297–358.

to be justified, for we already have been justified by faith. Rather, we do all things freely and joyfully for the sake of others.

St. Paul also circumcised his disciple Timothy, not because it was necessary for righteousness but rather to avoid causing offense to the Jews who were weak in faith and had not yet grasped the freedom that comes with trusting in Christ. However, when they despised faith's liberty and insisted on circumcision as a requirement for righteousness, Paul resisted them and did not permit Titus to be circumcised (Gal. 2:3). He did not wish to offend or scandalize those who were weak in faith, and thus Paul yielded to their practices for a time. But the Apostle also did not want to compromise the liberty of faith by yielding to those who stubbornly cling to works in order to justify themselves. He opted instead for a middle way, sparing the weak for a time while always opposing those who trusted in works. His goal in adopting this position was that all might be converted to the liberty of faith. This provides a good example for us to follow. We ought to accept and nurture the faith of those who are weak (Rom. 14:1), but we should resist boldly those who obstinately insist on works. We shall say more about this later.

We also have the example of Christ in Matthew 17:24-27, where the authorities sought to obtain taxes from the disciples. In this passage, Jesus discusses with Peter whether the sons of a king would be free from paying a royal assessment. Peter affirms that they would be free from such a tax, but notice that Christ still commands him to go to the sea, saying: "However, so that we do not give offense to them, go to the sea and cast a hook; take the first fish that comes up; and when you open its mouth you will find a coin; take that and give it to them for you and me." This story provides a wonderful illustration of the point we are trying to make. Christ refers to himself and his own as children of the king and thus in need of nothing. Yet he freely submits and pays the tax. Now, this work was not necessary for Christ's salvation. Nor do the works of his followers lead to righteousness. Rather, the works follow righteousness and are done freely with an eye toward serving others and providing an example of good works.

The counsel and advice of St. Paul in Romans 13:1-7 and Titus 3:1 also apply to this topic. He admonishes Christians to be subject to the ruling powers and be ready to do good works—not in order to be justified, for they are already righteous through faith—but that in the liberty of the Spirit they might serve the authorities and all others, obeying them freely out of love. The works of all clerical associations,[38] monasteries, and priests should be viewed in a similar manner. Each person should do the work dictated by his profession or station in life, not in order to obtain righteousness but to keep his body under control and to be an example to those who need to exercise a similar discipline over themselves. Of course, these works are done also to submit our will to the needs of others in the freedom of love. The greatest care must be taken so that a false confidence in works does not develop. Works do not justify or merit salvation. As I have said repeatedly, this is the result of faith alone.

Armed with this knowledge, any person can easily and without danger navigate his way among the infinite rules and laws of the popes, bishops, monasteries, churches, princes, and magistrates. Some foolish pastors insist that these mandates are necessary for righteousness and salvation, calling them "precepts of the church," but this is nonsense. A Christian, being free, will say instead: "I will fast, pray, and observe these human mandates, not in order to obtain righteousness or salvation, but in order to show respect to the pope, bishop, community, magistrate, and neighbor as well as provide an example for others to follow. I will do and suffer all things, just as Christ did and

---

38. Literally "colleges."

suffered far more for my sake though he needed nothing and was even subject to the law for me though he was not under the law." Although tyrants commit violence and injustice it will do me no harm as long as it is not contrary to God.[39]

From what has been said, everyone now has the tools to make the proper judgments on works and laws. They can also make trustworthy distinctions between pastors who are blind and foolish and those who are good and true. Any work that is not done exclusively to bring the body under control or serve the neighbor (as long as he or she does not request something contrary to God's will) is neither good nor Christian. As a result, I have a great fear that few, if any, clerical associations, monasteries, altars, and offices of the church are truly Christian in our day. This includes the special fasts and prayers on certain saints' days. To repeat, it is my fear that in all these things we seek only our own profit, believing that through these acts our sins are purged and salvation is attained. This way of things obliterates Christian freedom. It occurs because we are ignorant of the Christian faith and the abundant liberty that accompanies it.

Unfortunately, this ignorance and suppression of Christian freedom is encouraged by a large number of blind pastors. They agitate the people and persuade them to engage in these practices by praising these works and magnifying their importance by use of indulgences;[40] however, they never teach faith. So let

---

39. As this sentence indicates, Luther was not a political revolutionary. He was a conservative reformer who feared anarchy more than the unjust rule of a tyrant; however, the state has its limits. If it attempts to rule over matters of the soul it must be resisted. For example, in his treatise "Temporal Authority: To What Extent It Should Be Obeyed, 1523," he says that if a prince were to order that copies of the New Testament be confiscated, he should be resisted "on pain of losing one's salvation" (*WA* 11:266–67; *LW* 45:111–12). Nor was Luther a mere toady of the princes. He regularly railed against their arbitrary dictates and lavish lifestyles.

40. This is the first mention in "The Freedom of a Christian" of the controversy that ignited the Lutheran Reformation in 1517.

the reader be warned: if you wish to pray, fast, or establish a special fund in the church, I advise you not to do it to obtain a temporal or eternal reward. This would injure your faith, which alone offers you all things. Your one concern should be the enhancement[41] of your faith, whether it is disciplined by works or suffering. As for your gifts, distribute them freely and without consideration of gain. The goal is to have others benefit from you and your goodness. In this way you shall be truly good and Christian. What benefit to you are good works beyond those done to keep the body under control? Your faith is sufficient, through which God has given you all things.

This teaching tells us that the good we have from God should flow from one to the other and be common to all. Everyone should "put on" the neighbor and act toward him or her as if we were in the neighbor's place. The good that flowed from Christ flows into us. Christ has "put on" us and acted for us as if he had been what we are. The good we receive from Christ flows from us toward those who have need of it. As a result, I should lay before God my faith and righteousness so that they may cover and intercede for the sins of my neighbor. I take these sins upon myself, and labor and serve in them, as if they were my very own. This is exactly what Christ did for us. This is true and sincere love and the rule of a Christian life. And it follows that love is true and genuine where there is true and genuine faith. As Paul says of love in 1 Corinthians 13:5: "It does not insist on its own way."

In conclusion, as Christians we do not live in ourselves but in Christ and the neighbor. Otherwise, we are not Christian. As Christians we live in Christ through faith and in the neighbor through love. Through faith we are caught up beyond ourselves into God. Likewise, through love we descend beneath ourselves

---

41. Latin *augeatur*.

through love to serve our neighbor.[42] As Christians we always remain in God and in God's love. Christ says in John 1:51: "Very truly I tell you, you will see heaven opened and the angels of God ascending and descending upon the Son of Man."

We have sufficiently treated the topic of freedom. As can now be seen, we are speaking about a spiritual and true freedom, one that frees our hearts from all sins, laws, and commands. Paul says in 1 Timothy 1:9: "This means understanding that the law is laid down not for the innocent . . ." This freedom is above all other forms of freedom. The other types of freedom are external to a person. The difference between these two kinds of freedom is nothing less than the distinction between heaven and earth. May Christ grant us this freedom, both to understand and to hold for the future. Amen.

A Final Clarification

Finally, let us add a concluding word for those who simply fail to grasp something that has been clearly explained. Indeed, it is debatable whether or not they will even understand this additional explanation. There are plenty of people who hear us talk about the freedom of faith and immediately turn it into an opportunity to follow their own worldly desires and longings. They believe that all things are now allowed. They attempt to demonstrate their freedom by showing contempt for ceremonies, traditions, and human laws. It is as if their identities as Christians depended solely on the fact that they do not observe appointed days for fasting and abstaining from meat or that they refrain from the customary prayers. Their noses upturned, they scoff at religious regulations, but in actuality they end up

---

42. This should not be viewed in a condescending way. Rather, the incarnation of Christ becomes the model of life on this earth. Christians do not consider themselves "above" earthly life. Rather, this is precisely where their activity belongs.

diminishing all else that pertains to the Christian faith. The opposite extreme is found among those who rely solely for their salvation on their reverent observance of ceremonies, as if they would be saved because on the proper days they fast, abstain from meat, and offer the appointed prayers. They boast about the precepts of the church and of the fathers but have no grasp of matters central to our faith. It is evident that both sides are in error because they neglect the important things necessary to salvation while making noisy arguments about issues that are trivial and secondary.

How much better is the teaching of the Apostle Paul, who instructs us to take the middle way between the two positions mentioned above. He condemns both sides when he says in Romans 14:3: "Those who eat must not despise those who abstain, and those who abstain must not pass judgment on those who eat." In this passage you see that those who neglect or despise certain religious ceremonies—not out of a sense of piety but rather out of contempt—are reproved by Paul, who teaches us not to disparage them. Such people have an inflated sense of themselves because of their so-called knowledge. But Paul also says that those who advocate religious ceremonies are not to judge the other side. In the end, both sides neglect the love that builds up community. Instead, we ought to listen to Scripture, which teaches us not to go to the right or left (Deut. 28:14) but to follow the precepts of the Lord, which are just and lead the heart to rejoice (Ps. 19:8). It ought to be remembered that we are not made righteous by keeping or clinging to works or ceremonial rituals. But it also is true that we will not be counted as righteous because we neglect or despise them.

Our faith in Christ does not free us from works but rather from the foolish view that works result in our justification. Faith redeems, guides, and keeps our consciences so that we know our righteousness does not come from works. This does not mean works should be avoided. For example, our bodies cannot exist without food, drink, and all the other works needed to sustain them; however, our righteousness is not found in these activities but rather in faith. This does not mean, however, that the works of the body are to be despised or neglected. In this world we are bound by the needs of the bodily life, but we are not made righteous by them. Christ says: "My kingdom is not from this world" (John 18:36). He did not say, "My kingdom is not in this world." In 2 Corinthians 10:3 Paul says: "We live as human beings (walk in the flesh), but we do not wage war according to human standards." And in Galatians 2:20 he says: "The life I now live in the flesh I live by faith in the Son of God." Thus the works and ceremonies that are so much a part of our daily routines are done to meet the necessities of life and care for our bodies. We are not made righteous by these works but by our faith in the Son of God.

Given this situation, it is the duty of a Christian to take a middle path between these two types of people. On the one side, the inflexible and obstinate ceremonialists must be opposed. They are like deaf adders who are not willing to hear the truth of liberty (Ps. 58:4). Having no faith, they stubbornly insist on their own ceremonies as a means of justification. This is similar to the Jews[43] of old, who were unwilling to learn how to do the good. The people on this side must be resisted. In fact, even the opposite should be done, in bold and shocking ways, so that their ungodly views do not lead more people into error. In the presence of these people, one should feel free to eat meat, break fasts, and in the spirit of liberty given by faith, do things they consider to be the greatest of sins. Of them we should say: "Let them alone; they are blind guides of the blind" (Matt. 15:14). According to this principle, Paul would not circumcise Titus

---

43. The reference is to the New Testament portrayal of the Pharisees, whose concern for the letter of the law led them to miss its spirit.

when some of the leaders insisted that he should. Christ also defended the disciples when they plucked ears of grain on the Sabbath (Matt. 12:1-8). Many other examples could also be given.

On the other side of this issue are the simple-minded and ignorant. These are the ones Paul says are weak in faith. They are not able to grasp the meaning of the freedom given in faith—even if they wished to do so (Rom. 14:1). These are the ones we must take care not to offend. We ought to defer to their weakness until they have had the opportunity to become more fully instructed in the faith. They act the way they do only because their faith is weak. Therefore, fasts and other ceremonies they might think are necessary should be observed in order to avoid upsetting them. In this way we follow the command of love, which seeks not to harm but to serve. After all, they are not to be blamed for their weakness. It is their pastors who have used the tradition to take them captive. These ceremonies became like a rod that was used to beat the people. In fact, the teaching about faith and freedom should have been used to liberate the people from their pastors. Paul teaches us in Romans 14:21: "It is good not to eat meat or drink wine or do anything that makes your brother or sister stumble." He also states in Romans 14:14: "I know and am persuaded in the Lord Jesus that nothing is unclean in itself; but it is unclean for anyone who thinks it is unclean."

Accordingly, we must resist boldly those who teach the tradition in this way. Likewise, we must sharply criticize the laws of the popes, who use them to lead the people of God astray. At the same time, we must be patient with the large number of timid people who are held captive by these wicked tyrants and their manipulation of the laws until they are set free. Thus you should fight these wolves tenaciously but always keep in mind that the battle is for the sheep and not against them. This will happen if you attack the laws and the lawgivers while being careful at the same time to observe the laws with those who are weak so they won't be offended. This needs to be done until those who are weak recognize the nature of this tyranny and understand their freedom. If it is your desire to make use of your freedom, practice it in private, as Paul says in Romans 14:22: "The faith that you have, have as your own conviction before God." But be careful not to use this freedom in a way that offends the weak; however, in the presence of tyrants and other stubborn people, be firm and consistent in your use of this freedom. They need to know they are godless, that their rules and laws do not lead to righteousness, and finally that they had no authority to institute them.

We know that in this life we cannot live without ceremonies and works. Our young people are easily excited and untrained—they need to be restrained and saved from harm. Also, all of us need to keep our bodies under control by means of such efforts. It is evident that a minister of Christ needs to be wise, far-seeing, and faithful. They ought to guide and teach all Christians in these matters, being careful not to offend conscience and faith. As Paul warns in Hebrews 12:15,[44] they must take care "that no root of bitterness springs up and causes trouble, and through it many become defiled." In other words, these leaders must be attentive so that the people do not lose faith and accept the view that works justify. For faith must be taught constantly. Otherwise, the false opinions concerning works will prevail and many will be defiled. This is precisely what has happened as a result of the pestilent, godless, and soul-destroying traditions of our popes and the opinions of our theologians. These snares have trapped an endless number of souls and led them to hell. Indeed, we can infer from this the work of the Antichrist.

---

44. Luther assumes Hebrews was written by Paul, a view not shared by biblical scholars today.

In summary, as wealth is the test of poverty, the give and take of business the test of faithfulness, honors the test of humility, feasts and parties the test of temperance, pleasure the test of chastity, so ceremonies are the test of the righteousness of faith. Solomon asks in Proverbs 6:27: "Can fire be carried in the bosom without burning one's clothes?" Yet we recognize that we must live in the midst of wealth, business, honors, pleasures, and feasts. So, too, we must live in the midst of ceremonies and their accompanying dangers. For example, infant boys need to be cherished and cradled by young women in order to keep them from harm; however, when they are older it is possible for their salvation to be endangered by the opposite sex. Likewise, the untrained and excitable young people ought to be restrained and disciplined by the iron bars of laws and duties to keep them from falling into corruption. On the other hand, it would be nothing other than death for them always to think that following laws and rules[45] leads to justification. Much better if they are taught that being bound by these laws and rules is necessary to keep them from doing evil and to allow time for instruction in the righteousness of faith. But they need to know that they are not made righteous or gain merit by following these rules. Yet it is true that this teaching about the righteousness of faith would not endure unless their impulsiveness was restrained.

Thus ceremonies are to be given the same place in the Christian life that a model or plan would have for a builder or artisan. They are not meant to be the permanent structure, but without them it would not be possible to build anything at all. When the structure is finished, the plans are put aside. The point is not to despise the plans. Indeed, they are crucial to the project. What we do despise is the false estimate of them, since everyone knows they are not the real and permanent structure.

---

45. Latin *ceremonia*.

Imagine a person so incredibly foolish as to care for nothing in life other than the most expensive, careful, and meticulous preparation of plans but never to think of the building itself. What would people say about someone satisfied (or even boasting) with only the plans and models? Would not such a person's sanity be questioned and would not many judge it to be a waste of talent? Accordingly, we do not despise ceremonies and works. We regard them highly. But we despise the false value placed on works, which trap many into thinking that they are source of true righteousness. This is what happens to these hypocrites who spend their whole lives zealous for works but never reach the goal they are trying to achieve. Paul says of such people that they "are always being instructed and can never arrive at knowledge of the truth" (2 Tim. 3:7). They desire to build and even make plans, but they never get to the structure itself. They remain in the outward forms of religion and fail to taste its real power (2 Tim. 3:5). All the while they are pleased with their zeal and even judge others when they fail to see a similar pompous display of works. They have abused God's gifts and used them in vain. Had such people been filled with faith, they might have accomplished great things with regard to their own salvation and that of others.

Human nature and natural reason, as it is called, are inclined toward superstition and imagine that, when laws and works are prescribed, it must mean that righteousness can be obtained by following them. In addition, since this viewpoint is confirmed by the practice of all earthly lawgivers, it is impossible for them on their own to escape the slavery of works and comprehend the freedom of faith. Therefore, we need to pray that the Lord may mold or shape us as *theodidacti*, that is, those who are taught by God (John 6:5). In this way, God will write his law on our hearts, just as he promised to do. Otherwise, there is no hope for us. Only God can teach our hearts this wisdom hidden in mystery (1 Cor. 2:7). Human nature can only condemn this wisdom and judge it to be heretical. It is offended by it and regards it as foolish. This is what happened to the apostles and prophets in the Bible. A similar thing is happening to me and those like me at the hands of the godless and blind popes and their flatterers. In the end, may God be merciful to us and may God's face shine upon us, that God's way might be known on earth and his saving power among all nations. All praise to God, who is blessed forever.[46] Amen.

---

46. The end of the treatise, or benediction, is derived from Psalm 67:1-2.

ABBREVIATIONS

BC — *The Book of Concord.* Robert Kolb and Timothy J. Wengert, eds. Minneapolis: Fortress, 2000.

ER — *Encyclopedia of the Reformation.* Hans J. Hillerbrand, ed. 4 vols. New York and Oxford: Oxford University Press, 1996.

LW — *Luther's Works—American Edition.* 55 vols. Philadelphia: Fortress; St. Louis: Concordia, 1955–1986.

NRSV — New Revised Standard Version

WA — Luther, Martin. *D. Martin Luthers Werke: Kritische Gesamtausgabe. [Schriften].* 65 vols. Weimar: H. Böhlaus Nachfolger, 1883–1993.

WABr — Luther, Martin. *D. Martin Luthers Werke: Kritische Gesamtausgabe. Briefwechsel.* 18 vols. Weimar: H. Böhlaus Nachfolger, 1930–1985.

WATr — Luther, Martin. *D. Martin Luthers Werke: Kritische Gesamtausgabe. Tischreden.* 6 vols. Weimar: H. Böhlaus Nachfolger, 1912–1921.

FOR FURTHER READING

Forde, Gerhard. *Where God Meets Man: Luther's Down-to-Earth Approach to the Gospel.* Minneapolis: Augsburg, 1972. An introduction to Luther's thought by one of his masterful interpreters.

Kittelson, James M. *Luther the Reformer: The Story of the Man and His Career.* Minneapolis: Fortress Press, 2003. Remains the best one-volume biography of Luther in English.

Luther, Martin. *Faith and Freedom: An Invitation to the Writings of Martin Luther.* Preface by Richard Lischer. Edited by John F. Thronton and Susan B. Varenne. New York: Vintage, 2002. A fine collection of Luther's pastoral writings with a special emphasis on his sermons.

Luther, Martin. *Luther's Spirituality.* The Classics of Western Spirituality. Edited and translated by Philip D. W. Krey and Peter D. S. Krey. New York: Paulist, 2007. Contains a translation of the shorter German edition of *The Freedom of a Christian.*

Luther, Martin. *Martin Luther's Basic Theological Writings.* Edited by Timothy F. Lull and William R. Russell. 2d ed. Minneapolis: Fortress Press, 2005. The best single-volume collection of Luther's writings in English.

Paulson, Steven. *Luther for Armchair Theologians.* Louisville: Westminster John Knox, 2004. A thought-provoking overview of Luther's theology written for the general reader.

Veith, Gene Edward Jr. *The Spirituality of the Cross: The Way of the First Evangelicals.* St. Louis: Concordia, 1999. A helpful summary of Luther's theology with a particular focus on his theology of the cross.

GLOSSARY

Anfechtungen
A German word that describes the terror and despair Luther felt when he was unable to trust in God's goodness. It conveys a sense of being under attack and even cornered by a foe.

"The Babylonian Captivity of the Church"
Written by Luther in the pivotal year of 1520, a treatise in which he criticizes the Roman Catholic Church's understanding of the sacraments. Ultimately, he argues that only Baptism and Holy Communion should be considered sacraments.

Cajetan (1469–1534)
Also known as Cardinal St. Sisto. Influential leader in the Catholic Church at the time of Luther who was a noted scholar of the theology of Thomas Aquinas. Met with Luther in Augsburg in 1518 in an attempt to get him to retract his teachings.

"To the Christian Nobility"
A treatise written by Luther in 1520, the same year he wrote "The Freedom of a Christian." Among other things, it contains his argument for the "priesthood of all believers."

conciliarism
A movement to reform the church by means of a general council. Sometimes thought to be in tension with or in opposition to papal power.

Diet of Worms
A meeting in the German city of Worms in 1521, where Luther had a dramatic confrontation with the leading political and ecclesiastical authorities of the day. As a result of the proceedings, Luther was declared a heretic.

Eck, John (1486–1543)
Early and ardent foe of Luther. Debated with him in Leipzig in 1519 on the nature of the church's authority.

faith
For Luther faith encompassed the whole self and is best understood as trust. It included an intellectual dimension (the knowledge or "facts" of the Christian tradition), but it should not be understood as something limited to an activity of the mind.

Frederick the Wise (1463–1525)
The prince of electoral Saxony, the region in Germany where Luther lived. Frederick ultimately protected Luther against his various enemies.

Holy Roman Empire
In the sixteenth century, Germany did not exist as a nation. Instead, it was a collection of smaller states and principalities (roughly equal to the present borders of Germany) known as the Holy Roman Empire.

indulgences
A document saying that earthly (as opposed to heavenly) punishments due to sin had been forgiven. Widespread abuses occurred when the church authorized the selling of indulgences. This practice prompted Luther to write "The Ninety-five Theses."

justification
The situation of being in a right relationship with God. Luther argued that justification takes place by faith and not by works of the law.

Leo X (1475–1521)
Pope from 1513–1521. Author of the bull in 1520 that threatened Luther with excommunication.

Melanchthon, Philip (1497–1560)
Younger colleague of Luther at the University of Wittenberg, expert in biblical languages, and an important leader in the Reformation. Author of the Augsburg Confession (1530), one of the primary statements of faith for the Lutheran church.

Miltitz, Karl (1490–1529)
Papal ambassador who failed to forge a compromise between Luther and Rome in 1518–1519.

"The Ninety-five Theses" ✓
Luther's 1517 protest against the sale of indulgences. Printers made the Theses widely available in Germany and northern Europe.

"The Papacy in Rome"
Written by Luther in 1520, this treatise refutes the traditional papal claims to authority.

penance, sacrament of ✓
One of the seven sacraments in the Roman Catholic Church. Mandated annually, it involved confessing one's sins to a priest, hearing absolution, and then doing works of satisfaction according to the punishment merited by the sin.

Prierias (1456–1523)
Also known as Sylvester Mazzolini. Early opponent of Luther who defended the selling of indulgences.

righteousness
A quality possessed by God that is given freely to the undeserving sinner in the act of faith.

Roman curia
The body of bishops, councilors, and advisors that surround the pope. Most prominent members are the college of cardinals, who advise the papacy on the state of the church and who also elect a new pope in the event of a vacancy.

salvation
Has a future and a present-tense meaning. Salvation refers to the future state of blessedness that will be enjoyed by the saints in heaven. It also designates the present status of those who are in a relationship of faith.

The Small Catechism
Written by Luther in 1528 after he made a visitation of the churches in the Wittenberg area. It is designed to instruct people in the basics of the Christian faith.

"Treatise on Good Works"
Written by Luther in 1520. An extended sermon on the place of the commandments within an understanding of Christian freedom.

Wartburg Castle
Luther was spirited away to the Wartburg Castle after the Diet of Worms in 1521. This was a strategy of Frederick the Wise to buy some time for his beleaguered professor. While in the Wartburg, Luther translated the New Testament from Greek into German.

Wittenberg
City in Saxony that was the site of Wittenberg University and home of Martin Luther from 1512 until his death in 1546.

word of God
Has three overlapping meanings for Luther. First, it is the Bible itself. Second, it refers to Christ and in particular his death and resurrection. Third, it refers to the message preached about Christ and how his death and resurrection has liberated us from "sin, death, and the devil."